'COME ALL GOOD MEN AND TRUE'

Essays from the John B. Keane Symposium

'COME ALL GOOD MEN AND TRUE'

Essays from the John B. Keane Symposium

Edited by
Gabriel Fitzmaurice

CDERCIER PRESS

First published in 2004 by
MERCIER PRESS
Douglas Village, Cork
www.mercierpress.ie

Trade enquiries to COLUMBA MERCIER DISTRIBUTION,
55a Spruce Avenue, Stillorgan Industrial Park, Blackrock, Dublin

© The contributors

ISBN: 1 85635 435 0

10 9 8 7 6 5 4 3 2 1

Mercier Press receives financial assistance from
The Arts Council/An Chomhairle Ealaíon, Ireland

The publishers and Gabriel Fitzmaurice would like to thank The Gallery
Press, Loughcrew, Oldcastle, County Meath, Ireland, for permission to
quote Michael Hartnett's poems. Thanks also to Brendan Kennelly,
Leland Bardwell, Pecker Dunne and Áine Ní Ghlinn.

Printed in Ireland by ColourBooks Ltd.

Contents

Introduction

In July 2003, in my capacity as Director of Tarbert Education Centre, I helped to organise summer courses for National Teachers in Tarbert Comprehensive School. By far the most popular course – *ní nach ionadh*, it was organised in response to popular demand – was the course on English literature. It was titled, rather cumbersomely, 'Literature in the Locality: the Local Writer and the Curriculum as Exemplified in the Writings of John B. Keane', and it was centred on John B. Keane, the man and the writer. It took into account, among other things, his early years, his development as a writer, his place in Irish literature, particularly Irish theatre, approaching John B. Keane in the classroom and common themes in John B. Keane and Brendan Kennelly – two of the literary luminaries of North Kerry. Friends of John B. – actors, theatre producers and critics – delivered these lectures.

There were other lectures, equally lucid and thought provoking, to satisfy both the demands of the Department of Education and Science and the need to flesh out the lecture series as a course based on the 1999 Primary School Curriculum.

The series was a resounding success. Teacher after teacher came to us and told us how much they enjoyed and were enlightened – and enabled – by this approach to English literature. They wanted more.

As we cannot repeat ourselves by organising another John B. Keane course in the near future, we now do the next best thing: Tarbert Education Centre, in partnership with Mercier Press, publish the John B. Keane lectures. I hope you enjoy them as much as those who were fortunate to hear them originally at the seminar.

GABRIEL FITZMAURICE
Director, Tarbert Education Centre

'IS THE HOLY GHOST A KERRYMAN OR IS HE JOHN B. KEANE?'

Danny Hannon

I am seventy years of age and for sixty of those I knew, and have memories, of John B. Keane, and mostly good ones I am happy to say. I was at the National School with him in Listowel, and we were later at St Michael's College together. I was also lucky enough to have been involved in some of the major events of his life, and he is godfather to my eldest son. He also dedicated one play and one book to me, for which I am eternally grateful.

John was very close and private about his professional life, rarely spoke much about work in progress, never said anything critical about other writers, but as a public person he was very open and a man of great grace, manners and personal charm. He invited me to appraise some of his plays, and novels, when they were still in manuscript form. When he gave me a script, there were never any doubts about the ground rules; what he really wanted to hear was good news, he was not interested in criticism! 'When I give you this script,' he would say, 'I want your comment in one sentence; if you go on to a second sentence, I'll shut you up.'

I also have wonderful memories of driving him to opening nights around the country. He might have been uptight on the way there, but would always be mellow on the way home to Listowel, where we would drive around the laneways in the early hours, recalling his youth and the many characters he enjoyed. He loved to sing when he was relaxed. He was a nervous passenger but he was OK with me because we had so many shared memories of growing-up, and because I was a non-drinker, and, hopefully, a cautious driver. Surprisingly he didn't talk much on the way home about a play we had seen, and never ever thought about introducing changes; with John when it was over, it was over, and he was already thinking about his next play or novel. As a professional writer, he knew the value of words, and was always very concise with them. He would speak only briefly about directors and actors, and rarely commented on sets or lighting. In fact he was often more effusive after amateur productions, and would chortle all the way home after a good one.

I will concentrate here on what, I hope, will be a personal view of the man himself. In some ways my life was intertwined with his because I was involved with the Lartigue Theatre and had a bookshop and, ever since childhood, I was a great admirer of him. He was a very easy man to love, always a genuine friend. He was your quintessential Kerryman, brilliantly endowed with wit and humour. I don't believe any Irishman ever hit the hearts and minds of the Irish people like he did. He was also a splendidly generous person. I spent a number of years working in London, and when I returned to the family business, he drafted me into the Listowel Players, where I later had the privilege of co-producing (with Nóra Relihan) the great man himself in Arthur Miller's *The Crucible* and I directed him in one of the later productions of *Sive*. He was no problem to direct on stage, and took everything very seriously. With him in the cast, you could be sure of box-office success!

He was born in Church Street, Listowel, and the teaching profession was very much part of his life; his father was a teacher in Clounmacon school, a few miles outside Listowel; his brother, Dennis, taught in Dublin, and his daughter, Joanna, teaches in Tralee. He lived opposite another writer, Bryan Mac-Mahon, who was also the most famous national schoolteacher in the country at that time. In fact, Bryan taught John B. and they both had a high regard for each other's professionalism. You know how it is as you go through school, no matter what happens in life there is always that special relationship with your old teachers. All of his education was in the town of Lis-

towel, first in the old Boys' National School, and later in St
Michael's College, which was a little more tempestuous.

From his earliest days, he was a performer, never a silent
observer, always in the thick of things. When I was about six
or seven, he put on a concert in Jackeen Keane's loft, admis-
sion tuppence and this was so good that I can still remember
snatches of it. The audience were schoolboys, with J.B. acting
as master of ceremonies, and there were yodellers, magicians,
hypnotists and chancers. What I remember most was the raffle
– for a solid gold gent's wristlet watch, fourteen carat gold,
leather strap, guaranteed for life, tickets one penny each. I
remember it well because I won it, although the watch and I
never met – something about the Germans, Second World
War, spies, submarines and all sorts of complications – but
still I got two tickets for the next concert! I would love to
think that this was his first venture on stage – I'm sure it was,
and by a strange coincidence I can remember posters for one
of his later concerts, which said 'In aid of the Listowel EPA'
which he later explained, stood for The Empty Pockets Association. We all belonged to that outfit in those days!

If it was all Nash's lemonade and Geary's biscuits at the
National School, St Michael's College was a different ball-
game entirely. The curriculum was basic and classical, English and Irish, History and Geography, Latin and Greek and

Mathematics – four language subjects out of seven. This surely had a huge impact and inspiration on his career as a writer (and indeed on other writers also). Latin and Greek were dead languages, but what an incredible tapestry of history and legend they offered. We had daily encounters with all the Caesars, Euripides and Thucydides and that great storyteller, Homer. John was brilliant at St Michael's, articulate, bright, involved in every bit of commotion that was taking place. He was the leader of the pack, as they say. He tried to organise a college football team, campaigned for an extra half-day of studies and protested at the state of the toilets; he led other student crusades, most of which he lost on a head-to-head with the president of the college, and this ongoing conflict came to a dramatic confrontation in his last year at St Michael's. The president was a priest, a notorious bully whose legendary feats have been recorded elsewhere. He taught Greek with his fists and his feet and whatever sticks he could lay his hands on. He lashed and bashed us through the irregular verbs three days a week, and said, 'If you can master these, you need never fear anything in your life – except me'.

When John was in the Leaving Cert. class – where this priest also taught Elocution – the boys were asked to pick and read a poem. When his turn came, J. B. stood up and read a poem, and he was asked 'Who wrote this?' John said he wrote it himself, and the priest laid in to him. He bashed him and lashed him with his fists around the room.

Why? Who is to say? Did he think John hadn't composed it? Was he jealous? Did he think John was getting too smart or something? I'll tell you one thing, that day he lit a raging fire in John B. Keane that did not extinguish itself until a few years ago. He never ever got over that hiding. Most of us suffered at the hands of this teacher and got over it as the years went by. It was the same for everybody in the class; he didn't have any favourites, everybody was crucified in the same way. But it always surprised me that John never did. He was not a man to forgive and forget easily. I think it was probably more because of his sensitivity as a writer rather than the punishment. It is one of those strange quirks of fate that this poem – 'The Street' – is now on the school curriculum!

Recently as I was trying to put some focus on him, apart from his work, one thought struck me – no matter how great his achievements were as a writer, his personality was even bigger. That is strange in a writer, because we generally think of them as withdrawn, detached in their own little worlds with their pens and their plans. For instance comparing him to other writers like Brian Friel or Thomas Murphy or Martin Mc-Donagh, I think you would be hard-pressed to recognise their photos, let alone know anything of their personality. John had one of the most recognisable faces in Ireland, even at one time Fine Gael were considering him as a candidate for president of Ireland! That sort of recognition comes easily to politicians and sports people who are in the papers every day, but for a creative artist, living in a small town in the south-west of Ireland, far away from the media, it is extraordinary, and surely worth a study.

So, what made him such a giant of a personality? In two words, I would say 'media skills'. He really was an incredible performer, a super communicator, full of wit and humour, wisdom and compassion; he just could put a different angle on things and say things that made you think. He had a magnetic grip especially on radio and television, and had a huge impact on *The Late, Late Show*. He told me he never appeared with Gay Byrne without fortifying himself with a bottle of brandy! The ratings were always tops, whenever he was on, right through from the 1960s to the 1990s. Incidentally, when his play *The Field* was shown on television, it broke all viewing figures at the time. On radio, too he was in total control. I remember a Sunday morning, getting ready for Mass in Listowel in a bit of a rush, when I heard his voice on Radio Kerry. I stopped for a minute to listen and, half an hour later, I was still listening, enthralled, even though I had heard most of it before. The interviewer asked him one question and away he went without a pause for thirty minutes, he was riveting. No wonder he was in such demand at Montrose.

Maybe another reason why he had such a grip on the hearts and minds of Irish people was that he was a regular contributor to the papers. In the 1970s, he wrote a weekly column for *The Limerick Leader*, and he also wrote regularly in the *Irish Independent*. His columns were rarely about the rich and famous, more often about people whom he knew and loved, and they were seldom serious. One of his favourites was Jack Faulkner. Jack was one of the travelling community and was based in Glin, in west Limerick, but had family in Listowel, where he was a regular visitor to John's pub. Jack was a softly spoken charmer and he would regale everyone with his stories. The people of Glin were so enamoured of Jack that the Knight of Glin gave him a small plot of ground on his estate and the people of the village built him a lovely little house there. J. B. said to Jack, 'Do you ever meet the Knight of Glin?'

'Oh I do, I meets him regular.'

'And what would you say to him?'

'Well, when I'd see him in the daytime I'd say "good day, Knight", and when I'd meet him at night I'd say, "Good night, Knight".

John loved that story.

Another colourful character that he had great time for

was the famous Sonny Canavan who was a small farmer with a glass eye. He lived in a cottage out near Dirha Bog just a mile or so outside Listowel and Sonny was full of stories, very much into the old times, with a sharp wit that John admired. He was dramatic too, often he would go to the gents and leave his glass eye on the counter, and on returning would enquire of the eye, if anyone was talking about him in his absence! I remember going out with John to a Canavan Wren Dance one Christmas, out through the bog late at night and in the distance we could hear the bodhrán playing. We stopped and John said, 'Listen carefully, that's the beat of pagan Ireland coming up through the centuries, it must be kept alive'.

Sonny was a great character. He had a dog called Banana who featured in *The Limerick Leader*. Banana died and Banana II followed him, and the genealogy went on, like kings of England, to Banana IV. One of the litter could talk, another could sing, and one was silent, but Banana IV could both talk and sing! Frank Hall, who had a regular humorous programme on television, came down to do a piece on the great dog and his owner, on the understanding that the canine would attempt something operatic. They took all the paraphernalia, sound technicians and cameras and what have you, but when the great moment came, Canavan said, 'I'm sorry to disappoint you, but he says he has a bit of a head-cold and cannot do justice to his voice today'.

Probably, he rehearsed too much – you will not find Banana IV in the archives of RTÉ!

John rarely left the town of Listowel: he was rooted to it. He never liked to be away from home and family, or his beloved pub. Leaving the county was a huge trauma for him. He spent some time in England as a young man, like many of our generation, and he visited New York for a production of his play *Big Maggie*. I spent a famous week with him in London in the early 1970s – Mary, his wife, thought it would be a good idea for him to see some English plays. To the best of my knowledge those were the only three times he was outside the country. Those days in London were the most intense, traumatic, and nerve-racking days of my life! Living with him so closely for seven days, I thought the intensity of this man's life was incredible, he was wound up day and night. One day in particular, his literary agent in London had arranged for us to meet some theatre people, and we were in this pub in Chelsea where we met Elizabeth Taylor's bodyguard. This person could have been a film star himself – slim, trim, six-footer, twelve stone, immaculately dressed, and full of Hollywood stories. John drank about ten gins in the pub over a long lunch and having seen a play that night we ended up in a Notting Hill Gate club until about three in the morning. He was drinking solidly all that time – I figured he had something like twenty gins-and-tonics and when we returned to our hotel afterwards, thinking he must be feeling a bit unsteady, I held him by the elbow to help him up the steps, but he just took one look at me, brushed me aside and ran to the top! That was his style – he was his own man, independent even at three in the morning. My admiration for Mary Keane increased a hundred fold, because living with John B. must have been like living in a pressure cooker. Was I glad to get home!

Looking back over someone's life, your judgement is coloured and influenced by your most recent memories of them, but people change as they get older, and are much different to what they were in their earlier years. I think this is true of John, because his fame and fortune increased dramatically over the last twenty years of his life and he became more subdued and relaxed. By comparison, he was a different J. B. in the 1960s as he fought to establish himself as a writer, especially as he felt the so-called 'Establishment' was impeding his progress. They were a very powerful mafia and operated at different levels of Irish society, and they had colossal influence in the civil service and every government agency. J. B. was a liberal who cherished freedom, and abhorred abuse of power, and he had first hand experience of it. One of that brotherhood was the GAA who imposed a ban on playing 'foreign' games –

usually soccer and rugby. Not only could you not play the games, you couldn't even attend one of their socials. In one of his unpublished plays which we've been reading about lately – *The Vigilantes* – he shows an even darker side to the GAA: they would send men along, in motor-cars with darkened windows, to Landsdowne Road rugby matches, and if you were seen, you were suspended. He hugely resented this sort of kangaroo justice and intrusion into people's privacy. We formed a rugby club in Listowel, and I had the pleasure of playing with him in a few matches. For the record, he played at full back and he played rugby like he played Gaelic football! Mind you, it didn't matter – we were all suspended anyway.

His real *bete noir* was compulsory Irish. He had a deep love of Irish, but in those dark days there were numerous jobs that you could not get unless you had achieved a certain level in Irish. For instance if you wanted to become a beach guard in Ballybunion, you couldn't become one without a certain level of Irish! I remember he wrote an article in the *Irish Independent* called 'The Super Patriots' in which he had a go at the Irish-speaking, Gaelic football-playing, type of people. He highlighted the situation of a young soccer player from a Dublin slum, who didn't know a word of Irish, played soccer, and died patriotically for his country, and the UN, on duty in Cyprus. He was drawing the analogy between true patriotism and our 'super patriots' who were part of the establishment.

Not only John but also the vast majority of Irish people were against compulsory Irish. A Dublin architect, Christopher Morris, formed LFM (Language Freedom Movement), and we both joined; in fact, I became chairman of the Listowel branch. A public debate was arranged for The Mansion House in Dublin with Gay Byrne as chairman, and J. B. was one of the speakers. In favour of compulsion were Dónall Ó Móráin from Gael Linn, an tAthair Tomás Ó Fiaich (who later became cardinal) and Tomás MacGiolla, who was president of Sinn Féin. Boy was it an incredible night!

We were pure, innocent country boys, coming up from Listowel, who thought we were going to participate in a debate. Wrong! No sooner did John B. begin talking than chairs were hurled at him on stage, people were shouting from all corners of the room. It was chaos, the whole thing was disrupted, none of our speakers could be heard, and the abuse was horrendous. I tell you, it was an education for us to see how professional agitators could disrupt a meeting. Gay Byrne was staggered; he said next morning on the radio he couldn't believe that in Ireland such a thing would happen. Towards the end, it got scary; John B. said that a knife flashed on to the stage, and we all beat a hasty retreat to an Italian chip shop, with the help of our friend Garda Tony Guerin. Although the story has not lessened in the telling, the whole idea of compulsory Irish seems like long ago and faraway today, but that's how it was in the late 1960s.

Another arm of the same establishment was the Abbey Theatre, who famously rejected his first play, *Sive*, and his second, and he never forgave them for it, although they redeemed themselves in later years with some fine productions of his plays. I hasten to add that it wasn't out of charity, as they were huge box-office successes. Still, he softened in his attitude towards them and I was with him there when he was presented with the Gradam Award for distinguished Irish writers in 1998. He made a lovely speech recalling how life had changed for him professionally, and about one of his very early plays *No More in Dust* – which was performed at the Dublin Theatre Festival. One of the critics who went to see the play wrote in the *Evening Herald*, 'I don't know which play will win the award for the best play of the festival this year, but I've certainly seen the worst'. John continued: 'He was probably right!' It gives an idea of how much he had matured.

I will now give you a musical interlude. This is from a CD, a live recording in John B.'s pub:

'Will you give us a song, John?'

'I'll chance it, but from drinking beer last night I've a kind of a dry throat, unfortunately – but I'll try to sing anyway. It's a song about my native town and I've been trying to write it all my life and it was only lately, when I was walking along the river, that it came to me':

Oh sweet Listowel I've loved you all my days.
Your shining streets, your towering spires and and squares
Where sings the Feale its everlasting lays
And whispers to you in its evening prayers

Chorus

Of all fair towns few have so sweet a soul
Or gentle folk compassionate and true.
Where'er I go I'll love you sweet Listowel
And doff my distant cap always to you.

Down by the Feale the willows dip their wands
From magic bowers where soft the night wind sighs.
How oft I've strayed along your moonlit lands
Where late love blooms and first love never dies.

Chorus

Of all fair towns few have so sweet a soul
Or gentle folk compassionate and true.
Where'er I go I'll love you sweet Listowel
And doff my distant cap always to you.

He was a lovely singer, music was very much part of his life, and as you know he has some famous songs in his plays. I re-member being with him in the Cork Opera House for the opening night of his musical *The Roses of Tralee* which was a very lively piece of work. I'm surprised it hasn't been revived since, and that he didn't take on another musical.

In the early days of Writers' Week, I was programme director, and we were putting on an exhibition of the Lawrence Collection photographs of Listowel, taken in the 1890s. Seán O'Shea was hanging them on the walls of the Listowel Arms Hotel and he asked John to give a title to each picture. There was a photograph of Church Street but when it was being taken, a dog had walked across the street, and wagged his tail – the movement exaggerated the tail. I said to John, 'What will we title this one?'

'Church Street, with Famous Monkey Crossing'.

That was what I put up, and everybody believed it! He later expanded on the story in *The Limerick Leader*, saying a monkey had escaped from Duffy's Circus after a performance in Listowel, and was befriended by the locals. Subsequently he related the sad plight of a woman visitor to the town who complained to the gardaí that she had been bitten by a monkey and was looking for compensation, et cetera! He could keep stuff like that going forever!

I suppose no talk about him would be complete without mention of his friend Dan Paddy Andy, from Renagown, about whom he wrote books in both Irish and English. 'The man with the triple name' he called him. It has always amazed me that although John was an out and out 'townie' his knowledge of life in the country was staggering, and of course most of his work deals with the rituals of country folk, and their work, and people living on the margins of life, in the battle for survival in intimidating places like the Stacks Mountain. He had first-hand knowledge from summers spent in that area as a schoolboy. Dan Paddy Andy was the local matchmaker and many of J. B.'s works deal with this subject. Dan wore glasses that were like the ends of jam crocks, and he was drawing a pension for the blind. John tells the story that one day Dan was sitting in the cinema in Castleisland and he looked at the man sitting next him who happened to be the Blind Pensions Officer. Quick as a flash Dan asked him, 'Excuse me sir, but could you tell me if this is the bus to Listowel'. *Dan Paddy Andy – The Matchmaker* is a great history of a community very close to us, and not too many years ago.

Even allowing for John's summer holidays, and the fact that most of us are only one generation from the country, his intimacy with every aspect of rural Ireland mystifies me. I will illustrate this for you with a short piece from his novel *Durango*:

> *Early in the morning, Danny Dooley led the grey mare from the moist pasture at the rear on the haggard … Gently stroking the sensitive ears, Danny Dooley inserted the bit in the mare's mouth. He then placed the winkers, with reins already attached, over the*

head, then came the heavy collar which he slung with both hands
over the neck, then came the inelegant hames fitting perfectly into
the collar, then the straddle over the broad back and bound under the
abdomen with buckled strap, then the britching on the rump and the
band of the britching between thigh and point of buttock and at-
tached to the straddle again with the strap and buckle, then the reins
through the rings of the hames ...

And on it goes with bellybands, hooks, traces, and all the rest. I think it is a beautiful description of how to tackle a horse, and it proves my point about his knowledge of country affairs. Read the book, you will enjoy it.

I would like to quote a poem dedicated to John B. for you. To celebrate John's fiftieth birthday, Mercier Press brought out a book called *Fifty Years Young – A Tribute to John B. Keane*, a celebratory collection of reminiscences about him, and here is Ray MacAnally's tribute:

There's bonfires on the hillside,
There's cheering in the glen,
John B. is celebrating
The two score years and ten.

Twenty years of poetry
And twenty years of plays,
And a new book on the market
Every ninety days ...

God the Son is worried,
With a sense of cosmic guilt,
Because he hears in Heaven's halls,
The dancing Kerry lilt.

'Almighty Da,' he says, 'you know
The secrets of the soul
Is the Holy Spirit biased
In favour of Listowel?

'An awful thought has struck me,
Almighty Da serene –
Is the Holy Ghost a Kerryman,
Or is he John B Keane?'

And that is it – all you ever wanted to know about John B
Keane but were afraid to ask! I hope it gives you a small in-
sight into the man. He was a loyal and generous friend. Even
being close to him I was always in awe of his talent. At times,
I had problems in my life, and he directed me wisely. Typi-
cally, when he gave you advice, it was always in one sentence,
and was always perfect, always original. He was the most courageous person I have known. In his last three years, he suffered greatly from that dreadful prostate cancer. Yet he never
once mentioned it, never complained, rarely mentioned his
treatment – even though I often saw the suffering in his face.
To the very end, he was the same J. B.; the body might have
been weak, but the spirit was indomitable. In my funeral ora-
tion, I said everything he touched had the lustre of pure gold.
And that is what he was, a treasure.

John B. Keane and the Ireland of his Time

Fintan O'Toole

In Memoriam John B. Keane

New Ireland holds you were of Ireland Past,
An Ireland that was changing as you wrote,
That you didn't move with Ireland that was fast
Changing from the times we took the boat
To be Paddies in an England where we'd slave
For a bedroom and a few pints down the pub;
Ireland of the navvy's in its grave,
We've money now where once we used to sub.
'He didn't move with Ireland': let those who
Follow fashion take thought for today;
As Ireland lost its past, a poet, you knew
The timeless things: you wrote them plot and play.
You didn't move with Ireland. No! You stayed
With the primal heart where all true drama's played.

Part of what I wanted to say is in a sense a response to a poem
of Gabriel Fitzmaurice's called 'In Memoriam John B. Keane'.
It's interesting that Gabriel should say that the poem is partly
an agreement and partly a disagreement with something I'd
written because what I want to say this morning is, in turn,
partly an agreement and partly a disagreement with that poem.
I want to reflect on some of the issues that the poem raises
because I think it goes to the heart of some important questions about John B. Keane, about contemporary Ireland, but

also about the nature of theatre itself. It raises the whole question of how much a work of theatre relates to its times, how much is it a prisoner of its times? How much should we look for the specifics in trying to explain a play through the circumstances of its creation? And how much does it escape from those circumstances and leave them behind?

I think, to start perhaps a little abstractly, theatre is a form of art which is very much tied up with time in a number of different ways but the most obvious one is that theatre is a form of art which unfolds in time. You may say, 'well, doesn't every piece of art do that, whatever its form?' and, yes, of course, to a certain extent it does. But I think theatre has a very specific relationship with time – what a piece of theatre does to us is that it imposes its own time-frame on us.

If you read a book, for example, you read it in your own time, you set the pace, you decide 'I'm going to read ten pages now, I'm going to leave it, I might not come back to it for another week, I might skip over a bit, I might re-read a piece'. The reader sets the pace. If you look at a painting on the wall, something quite similar happens. You decide how much time you're going to spend, you decide how you're going to allocate that time. Are you going to spend five minutes looking at a piece of detail on a woman's glove in a portrait, or are you going to stand back and look at the whole thing for thirty seconds and then move on and look at something else? The time-frame again is set very much by the person who experiences it. It is even increasingly true with film or television as we view things on DVD or video, and overturn the creator's time-frame by using fast forward and re-wind buttons, freeze-frame and pause.

Theatre, and this is something it shares very much with music, is a form of art in which we as the audience do not in fact set the rules for how time unfolds; we are prisoners of the unfolding time which is being spooled out on stage, as it were. That is why theatre sometimes, when it's bad, is the worst of all art experiences. There is a quality of boredom in the theatre which is much worse than, say, the boredom in the cinema, because it is unfolding at a pace which we cannot control at all and therefore if what is happening is not engaging us, it can be absolutely excruciating. We feel trapped and imprisoned.

And yet at the same time it's also one of the reasons why, when it works, a piece of theatre is an extraordinary experience – because we do, to an extent, leave our own time, our own sense of our own lives unfolding at a certain pace, and enter into another time, the time which is set by the writer or the actors and the technical crew and everybody who has been involved in the production. And that experience is central to the way in which we approach theatre.

There is a line in Tom Murphy's play, *The Gigli Concert*, which I think sums up the existential nature of a piece of theatre itself. One of the characters says to the other: 'You and I are alive in time at the same time'. And the experience of theatre is the experience of being alive in time – at the same time as the people on the stage. We enter into the pace of their lives and that pace takes over and takes us out of ourselves. That's quite central to the transformative nature of good theatre. You feel, after a very intense piece of theatre, that something has happened to you which is out of the ordinary and that sense of being out the ordinary is very much tied up with a slight warp in the normal continuum of time as we usually experience it.

If that's true, it raises quite interesting questions about the way in which we talk about theatre and its times. How much do we become prisoners of an experience which is unfolding in the present – which, after all, a piece of theatre is: theatre only has one tense, which is the present tense. Of course theatre is not the words on the page which were written by John B. Keane in 1958 or 1959; theatre is the experience you are having at the moment when you are there present in the theatre with a play like *Sive* which is unfolding before you.

So how much then do we engage in that sense of a kind of continual present in the theatre? How much do we nevertheless have to be conscious of the circumstances of what this play meant when it was created? And come to that, what were the circumstances of its creation? Can we understand the play properly without thinking our way back into the past, and into the world that created this piece of work just as much as the particular writer did?

John B. Keane is a particularly interesting case through which to think about all of this because one of the differences between a good piece of theatre and a mediocre one is that mediocre theatre often has a very simple sense of time. It just happens, it unfolds, it's over and then you're gone. Whereas really interesting pieces of theatre exploit one of the capacities that theatre as an art form has, which is that it can do more than one thing at the same time. Again, unlike a piece of prose or unlike a painting, theatre, because it's happening in front of us, can actually be very complex in the way it deals with narrative and with what's being presented. You can have two quite different worlds on stage at the same time, you can have at least two different things happening at any one moment. And that's really what makes the form interesting and allows it to survive, perhaps long after it was thought to have died: it's been superseded technologically by television or film and yet it still remains a very vital form for us.

That sense that there may be two worlds on stage is a way of approaching this whole question raised by Gabriel's poem of: did John B. Keane move with the times? Is he a reflection of the 1950s? Does he cease to speak to us as we move further and further away from that period? To put it another way, you can approach Keane's work through the question: is there more than one time-frame in any one moment in his plays? And I would suggest that what you find is that when the answer to that question is yes, you're dealing with very powerful Keane work and when the answer is no, you're dealing with much less powerful Keane work, or certainly much more problematic Keane work.

Keane clearly is at one level an extraordinarily accurate and acute reflector of his own times and the circumstances in which he began to write. It's not accidental and we should never forget that there is an extraordinary flowering of theatrical writing in Ireland in 1958, 1959 and 1960. A whole generation of extraordinary playwrights comes into being, finds its voice, at precisely that time. This is something we can sometimes take for granted and forget how really genuinely extraordinary it is, that within five years you have the first works of Tom Murphy, Brian Friel, John B. Keane, Thomas Kilroy and Hugh Leonard. You can say, well, that was pure coincidence, that we just happened to have this group of young men in disparate places in Ireland ranging from Donegal to north Kerry, and from Dublin to Tuam, all beginning to write extraordinary plays at the same time. And maybe it is just coincidence, maybe it's just the way life is sometimes. But I think it is much more likely that there is something in the air, that there is a moment when it becomes possible for a certain kind of mind to articulate theatrically a sense of what is going on at a deeper level in Irish society at that time. Because this is a time not just when you get a number of extraordinary theatrical writers but that you get a form which is extraordinarily unusual in theatrical history, and that form is tragedy. There are very few periods in theatrical history when successful tragedy has been written. I don't mean just one tragedy but when you've had a series or sequence of tragedies produced within a concentrated period of time (and you really are talking about the Greeks) you're talking about that astonishing period in the 1590s and early 1600s, and you're not talking about very many other periods in theatrical history. But you are talking about Ireland in the late 1950s and early 1960s and the fact that not just a range of writers, but a particular, highly unusual form, begins to flower in that place at that time. I think that cannot be coincidental. There has to be something else going on which is a relationship to that particular society.

So, what is that something, and what is it in relation to Keane in particular? Because Keane seems to me to have produced in that period a number of plays which are genuinely tragic. They're not just melancholic or sad or grim, they are tragic in the full sense, in the Greek sense, in the Shakespearean sense, *Sive* being one of them, *The Field* and *Big Maggie* being two others. So why does Keane produce tragedy, and why is that part of a broader movement that's happening around him culturally and socially?

Tragedy is a form that becomes possible when there are two worlds existing at the same time and it's a theatrical form because, as I said, theatre is at its best when there are two worlds on stage at the same time. What I mean by saying two worlds are coexisting is that there are two worlds morally, ethically, socially, culturally; there are two ways of understanding the world, two human frameworks, two sets of terms of reference for how we should live, which have equal weight and which therefore trap people within the no man's land or no woman's land between the two of them. It's not unusual for there to be different ideas around the place – all throughout human history there have always been people who have had arguments about what the right way forward is, what the right way to think is, what the right way to act is – that's not what produces tragedy. What produces tragedy is when there's a moment of balance between two different frames of reference whereby in a sense it's possible for somebody to believe that both of them are right and therefore it becomes impossible for someone to behave in a way which is in fact right.

You can explain it in terms of someone like Macbeth, to take a Shakespearean example. Macbeth behaves appallingly according to the codes of feudal medieval society. He commits three horrendous breaches of the deepest and most fundamental ethical codes of his time, and of course he says this very explicitly, he knows this: he murders Duncan, who is his king, who is his kinsman, and who is his guest and the tragedy of Macbeth is about the fundamental nature of that breach. At the same time, however, we can watch the play as being more than just a play about a psychopath who breaks taboos because we also have a sense that there is a different set of values that is beginning to emerge which is an ethic of individualism, an ethic of ambition, an ethic where somebody like Macbeth is also drawn to the idea that your personality, your sense of yourself is not governed simply by the rules of medieval society but you can actually invent yourself, you can make a life for yourself, you can decide what your fate should be – which is I suppose, whether we approve or not, a modern notion. It's partly because that's what's going on in Shakespeare's time that it is possible for him to create tragedy. And I would say, equally, if you look at *Sive*, the reason why it is a tragic play in that same sense is you also have these two completely different world views playing themselves out on stage at the same time as the story is being told.

I think if you look at Garry Hynes' recent production of *Sive*, one of the interesting things it does is that it stops treating Mena, who is the wife in the house, the woman who sells Sive, like an ogre, or as some kind of emanation from a medieval darkness. It treats her as a perfectly understandable and indeed in some ways admirable modern woman. After all, what Mena's trying to do in the play is something that everybody in Ireland aspired to at the time – she wants an ordinary life, an ordinary family.

One of the huge transformations that was taking place in Ireland around the 1950s and into the 1960s was a fundamental change in the nature of the Irish family. Up to the 1960s, the typical Irish family was an extended family, a family which included a much wider sense of kinship than the modern typical western European and American nuclear family – Mammy, Daddy and the kids. It was quite typical for families to have more than two generations: you often had grannies and granddads living in the house, you may have had maiden aunts, old bachelor uncles around the place. The sense of family, the sense of kinship was very different. If you look at the household of *Sive* at the beginning of the play it is a traditional extended family in that sense: you have Mena and her husband, Mike, whom we would normally expect to be the centre of a nuclear family but they're not. The child in the house, Sive, is not their child but the child of the dead sister. The oldest person in the house, the old woman, is seen by Mena as a burden, as somebody who is not welcome, who is part of this extended family structure. And really, all Mena wants is what would in modern Ireland, in 1960s Ireland, be the norm: she wants to have a nuclear family. She wants to get rid of the young girl and the old woman, to have herself and her husband start their own family and to be able to build a modern Irish nuclear family. She wants to be a modern Irish woman. However much we may be horrified at the methods she adopts in order to achieve this, the sort of cruelty she gets trapped in, what makes her tragic is that there is a sense in which she is behaving according to a certain standard of ethics. She's not a monster; she's just trying to get something which people around her are beginning to regard as the norm and as a good thing.

And yet, of course, there is this other world, the world of extraordinarily old, deep values which is represented strongly by the travelling people. They come in and declare blessings and curses, a very ancient and profound sense of right and wrong which is tied up with a notion of the sacred – with what I suppose you can only describe as a pagan world whereby things are either holy or unholy, are either sacred or profane, where there isn't room for the kind of subtle social shift that Mena is trying to engineer.

And Mena is a tragic figure because she is caught between two worlds: she's caught between two ways of behaving, two ways of understanding how families should operate, how relationships should operate, what people should aspire to. She wouldn't be tragic if she were either one or the other. If she were simply a cruel-hearted modern bitch, she would not be a tragic figure. If she were simply someone who was a superstitious emanation from a dark pagan past, she wouldn't be tragic. She's tragic because she has a foot in both camps, she exists simultaneously in both worlds, and therefore in a sense nothing that she can do will be right.

In the same way if we think about the Bull McCabe in *The Field*, you have again a changing society which produces two worlds. The focus here is not family but property, different ideas of property. As far as the Bull is concerned, he is right, he is acting according to the way in which people should act. He has worked that field, he has cleared the stones, he has put his life into it and therefore by an older idea of property that field is his. To him it is an injustice and an outrage that it should be taken from him and that it should be treated as a commodity which can be sold to an outsider. And again, it's not accidental that the outsider is someone who wants to use the field for industrial purposes. In the original version of the play – though this isn't nearly as clear in the film and the way it was subsequently interpreted – the symbolism of the field itself lies between agriculture and industry. The new man coming in wants to buy the field, wants to use it as a quarry, and wants to see it as a commercial resource which can be used in a modern industrial Ireland. The Bull sees it as a part of an ancient agricultural heritage, which is his. So, it's not just that there are two ideas of property; these ideas also in turn represent two different worlds, two different views of what Ireland should be like. And, of course, this is exactly the time at which this is the key question in Irish society. You could argue that the first great work of the second Irish dramatic renaissance is not a play at all but is T. K. Whitaker's document, *Economic Development*, which was published in 1958 by the Department of Finance. It said 'Look, we've tried being a traditional enclosed society and it hasn't worked because everybody is leaving so we've got to shift to become a modern industrial urbanised society.' The whole set of changes that's happening in the big world of Irish politics, society and economics at that time is shaping the concerns of the playwrights, and I think Keane very much among them.

Keane is extraordinarily astute about all this. As a student of this society, he senses exactly how people are caught between one way of understanding the world and another; it seems to me that he is incomparable. Even if you were a sociologist or an economist wanting to understand what was going on in Ireland at that time you would have to look at those plays. They contain at one level an extraordinarily brilliant description, which is anthropological, sociological, or whatever you want to call it, of a mentality at that time and the way in which people are caught.

The question though is, is that all the plays are? Because if it is, then no matter how sociologically interesting they may be, they will cease to be of any great relevance in the theatre. As we move away from that time, as we move away from that sense of a tragic balance that was there at the time, the plays will probably make less and less sense to us. So the question then is, is there another time scale, is there something else going on, is there a level of these plays that is not directly concerned with the Ireland of their times at all but is about something else? It seems to me that in at least some of the plays there is and this is why I think they will survive beyond the particular concerns that gave birth to them.

One of the things going on is a sense of form. We don't

read Shakespeare now to understand the dynamics of mentalities as people moved from feudalism to an industrial society, we read them because of their extraordinary dramatic tension. We don't read the Greek plays to understand the tension between a rising individualism in Athens in the fifth century BC and an older traditional notion of the gods and faithfulness to the old ways. Even though that is one of the things that's going on in the plays, we read them because of their extraordinary tension, the form, the drama, the pressure that comes out of the tension. It seems to me that, in the same way, one of the things that will make the best of Keane's work survive is that in the theatre the reasons for the tension become irrelevant and it's the tension itself – the pressure of what unfolds – which actually issues forth in something that holds our attention and engages us and involves us.

I think there is something more explicit in Keane's work where he's dealing with this sense of coming out of different worlds in a way which is actually not specific to time at all but has a much broader and deeper relationship to things. I hesitate to use the word 'timeless' because I think it's often an abused word, but they are certainly universal and relate to the human condition in ways that don't really require an understanding of the specific economics or social politics of Ireland in the mid- or late-1950s for their appreciation.

I think what we can say about Keane is that at his best there are not just tensions in the plays between different mentalities but that there are two wholly different time-frames working in the plays themselves. There is a time-frame which is short, specific and immediate, if you like the sociological time-frame, and that is very strongly present and very explicit in a lot of the work. But there is also a time frame which is mythic, which comes out of a mythic view of the world and which is not at all specific to particular circumstances. And I think we can go slightly further and say that when Keane's work doesn't fully achieve that sort of status and have the same kind of power on the stage that it needs to have, it's because there's not quite that same sense that these two time-frames are unfolding simultaneously.

Maybe one of the ways of getting at this is to look briefly at a counter example, an example of a play which I think is extraordinary, which I still want to see being done on the stage a whole lot more – but ultimately still seems not to work completely as a work of theatre – *Sharon's Grave*. Keane wrote this play very much in the same time, in the same circumstances as *Sive* and yet I think it is a more problematic play and in some ways an even more powerful play, at moments.

Sharon's Grave is particularly striking because it's one of the few Keane plays from that period where there is a specific date given. *Sive*, for example, is described in Keane's notes as 'taking place in the recent past', which is a wonderfully elusive description of the time. Does he mean in the recent past of 1959, which would place it maybe around 1954, 1955? Or does he mean that this is to be interpreted as the recent past any time you produce the play, so if you produce the play in 2003 does it mean 1995? Probably not, probably what he has in mind (I think it's fairly clear from the circumstances of the play) is the recent past as of 1959 but I think it's interesting that he is deliberately elusive about that. With *Sharon's Grave* he tells us exactly when the play is set – he says 1925 – and it's one of those things you don't pay much attention to when it's on stage but if you read the play then you're looking at it thinking '1925?' I was reading it again recently, I was actually quite surprised to see that there is a specific date on it because if you read the play there is absolutely nothing in the substance of the play that is 1925, it's not specific to 1925 at all. I mean, 1925 is a fairly interesting and specific period: you have a new state emerging, you've just had a civil war, you've just had a war of independence, it's not as if it's a quiet, unremarkable time in Irish history. Yet, one of the obvious absences is that there's absolutely nothing in *Sharon's Grave* which refers at all to the events that would have been fresh in people's minds in 1925. If you think about the contemporary plays in

1925–1926, you have *The Plough and the Stars*, which is still the great play of that time, and it's still absolutely and utterly bound up with the events of 1916, and with the aftermath of the foundation of the state. It is very much imbued with a very particular sense of place and period. Whereas *Sharon's Grave* giving you a specific time only draws attention to the fact that this time that is given to you is almost completely irrelevant. I think it is safe to say that there is nothing in *Sharon's Grave* that could not happen in exactly the same way if it was set in 1825 or 1725. Even if it were set in 1925 BC, would you have to tell the story differently? I think the answer is – no, you wouldn't. There's almost nothing in the play either in terms of what happens, the technology of what happens, the things people have in the house, the implements that are used, the props that are used, that could not have been placed at almost any time in human history. We can go even further I think and say almost any place in human history before the modern world. The only thing that really places it in time is that it is pre-industrial, it's pre-modern, it's before urban industrial society; you certainly couldn't have *Sharon's Grave* set in Temple Bar in Dublin in 2003. But beyond a certain point at which society has become industrialised this play could be set in Botswana in 1000 AD, it could be set in Hungary in the year of our Lord – you could imagine it unfolding at any time. And the reason for that is that in fact the time-frame of the play is entirely and explicitly mythical.

John B. actually describes the play in a programme note for one of the more recent presentations of it as 'a struggle between a sex-crazed delinquent and an upright young man whose heart is pure'. You can't imagine a more clear and perhaps crude opposition working its way through a drama: you have on the one side the sex-crazed delinquent and on the other hand you have the upright man whose heart is pure, and that's what the play is about. I don't think he had his tongue too firmly in his cheek when he used that description.

In a way, one of the big problems of producing *Sharon's Grave* now is that it relies on an identification between the way people look and the way they are in their hearts, which I think is actually quite objectionable to us now. If you think about the fantastic events of the Special Olympics, one of the things we're learning as a society is not to jump to conclusions about people's moral status or intellectual status or spiritual status by how they look and how they seem to us. We no longer think it is right to judge disabled people as stupid or evil or nasty, and that is one of the great achievements of our civilisation. Yet, *Sharon's Grave* is a play which really depends quite fundamentally on making a very clear association between the physical disability of the evil character, the sex-crazed delinquent, Dinzie Conlee, and his delinquency. He is a nasty character, in many ways, because we see him on stage as a twisted cripple and we understand from the moment he gets carried onto stage on the back of his brother that he is twisted both physically and spiritually. The identification between the physical and the moral is not even a metaphorical process; it's almost a process of complete transference.

To emphasise this point, the actual stage description of Dinzie in the printed version of the play reads as follows:

> *They are two people, one carrying the other on his back. The man on the back moves and looks craftily over the other's shoulder, watching for movement in the room. The other looks stupidly about. The man on his back is Dinzie Conlee. The man carrying him is his brother, Jack Conlee. Dinzie Conlee is of indeterminate age. His face is gruesome, twisted as he looks about. He is slightly humped, a wizened small person, his legs paralysed. The man, Jack Conlee, on the other hand is a large, well-cut, well-proportioned man in his early twenties.*

Immediately when you see this extraordinary creature coming in, which is this kind of two-backed beast, you are in a world where this means that Dinzie is an evil spirit. It is a pagan world. It is a world which is very much pre-Christian in the sense that it makes those kinds of assumptions which pagan societies often make – if somebody is ill, if they are deformed, it's a judgement of the gods on them, they are unclean and they are a threat to the community.

It's a real problem. In a way *Sharon's Grave* is a bit like *The Merchant of Venice*: it's very difficult to produce *The Merchant of Venice*, it's a hugely problematic business, because how do you deal with the elements of anti-Semitism which are clearly in the play? Can you present a Jew as somebody who is cruel, who is heartless, and who is determined to get his revenge on the gentile community? If so, how do you do it? Likewise, how do you present Dinzie Conlee on the stage? The obvious way to do it would be to say, well let's forget about the fact that he's a cripple, let's not have him twisted, let's have him walking around the stage and being a good-looking young man. But the problem is that if you do the play collapses entirely because it actually does depend on that opposition of handsome and pure on the one side to ugly and degenerate on the other, because it is mythic, because its governing mentality is a powerful evocation of the way in which people thought about the world probably from time immemorial until an extraordinarily recent period in history when we stopped making those kinds of connections.

Almost at the start of *Sharon's Grave* you have this character, Neelus, the simple brother in the house, who describes a mythic story and he tells the mythic story which is connected to 'Sharon's Grave'. It is a swallow-hole which is very close to the house and into which Sharon, the princess, is alleged to have been dragged by her evil companion in some sort of mythic time, and this curse will not be broken until a beautiful, handsome young man and a twisted, evil man fall into the grave as well. That's actually the story of the play. It's not George Eliot, it's not even *Sive*, and it's not a sociological play. There's no sense in which if you try to understand it as being play about a certain society that you get anywhere with it at all. The only way to produce a play like that is to take it completely on its own terms and to present it as a work of myth, as something that in fact could have been written at the time of Aeschylus or Homer and stand back from it morally and ethically and not make the kinds of judgements that most of us want to make about it, saying, 'well, you can't actually put someone on stage who is physically disabled and assume that because they're physically disabled they're also a nasty person'.

However, it's not just an ethical problem with *Sharon's Grave*, it's also a theatrical problem: it is very, very difficult to present a play like that without going over the top. It is what we would normally think of as an extraordinarily melodramatic piece of work. The action of the play is extremely vivid, violent and disturbing. It's sexually driven in a most explicit way: it's an extraordinary play to have come out of what was supposed to be a conservative, buttoned-up society in 1960 when it was first produced. It's a play where sexuality is rampant, uncontrolled and dangerous. It's very explicitly stated in the play: it is said to the young woman in the house that her father is dying, she only has the simple brother who is going to be locked away in a home, but if she's left alone in the house she will be raped. This is stated absolutely clearly and explicitly. It's a world in which if there was a woman on her own it was assumed that she would be attacked, that there is this kind of mad, violent, uncontrolled male sexuality as a sort of primeval satanic force which has taken over these people and cannot be contained or controlled in the normal webs of human contact or behaviour. The family doesn't exist much in a play like this. It therefore seems to refer to a world where there was no enlightenment, no sense of spiritual or ethical morality coming into play, where there's no sense of Christian superstructure having been imposed on the world. You can say in a simple sense that obviously this refers to stories that Keane gathered in Lyreacrompane and which were still alive in Ireland of the 1950s but at some level that is almost irrelevant to it. He could just as easily have taken these stories from any part of the world at any period before modernity.

So, you get an extraordinarily melodramatic conclusion to this play where the nice, simple but handsome and morally upright young man carries off the evil spirit of Dinzie Conlee on his back and they jump down the hole and the story is fulfilled. Yet it's a deeply disturbing and resonant piece of work, even in bad productions, because it seems to speak to us out of the darkness that is perhaps still within us at some level and that goes well beyond our notions of culture or society or history. It seems like something that has come up out of the ground, it's almost like an evil spirit in itself. It comes out of a pagan world, and what characterises that kind of world is that it's not historical, it is not a mentality which has a chronological sense of history but rather is mythical, it has a sense that these stories tell themselves over and over again, and they inflict themselves on humanity.

At one level therefore if you take *Sharon's Grave* as a counter-example at one extreme, at the other you have stuff like *The Chastitute,* which is I suppose a kind of whimsical take on a certain kind of Irish person and a certain kind of Irish mentality which Keane would have been familiar with from the 1950s. But when it's presented in the 1970s it seems sort of nostalgic and without any great force because it's simply an attempt to nostalgically recapture a certain world which he knows is dead and has no mythic uplift whatsoever in it. And actually that kind of work – and I think there are a number of later Keane plays in this category – it seems to me will not last at all and perhaps shouldn't last. Because all you have, in a sense, is Keane the social observer without Keane the pagan mythologist. But if you take that to be the case – if you say well yes there are starkly different kinds of failure of which Keane is capable – it perhaps comes closer to explaining his uniqueness than a simple sense of saying 'John B. Keane is wonderful and everything he does is great'. A writer who is capable of very, very different kinds of failure is an extraordinarily rich writer. Most writers who fail, do so usually for the same reasons – because of the same blind spots or difficulties in their own view of the world or their control of the material that they have. Keane fails in such starkly different ways – myth without society or society without myth – that he reminds us of the extraordinary nature of his successes.

What you actually get with his best work is a sense of balance between these two very, very different visions: a vision which is acute and sociological and very much of its time and place on the one side, and a vision which is dark and mythological and pagan on the other side, which is not simply of a different time but in a sense is of no time at all. When those two things come together, as I think they do in plays like *Sive* and *Big Maggie* and *The Field*, you get something which is the hallmark of great theatre: two worlds on the stage at the same time. You have that sense of an extraordinary richness and the kind of pressure and tension which emerges out of watching people's stories unfold as they attempt to walk a line between two incompatible ways of thinking and being and feeling and understanding.

That's the point of tragedy: it's tragic not because someone has a flaw within themselves or because they just didn't get it right. What makes something tragic is that it could not be right, that there is no way in which this story could have been changed, that you couldn't at some point just have said, 'let's not do that, let's do something else and everything will work out happily'. There are plays and stories in which that happens and they may be wonderful in their own way but they're not tragic. Tragedy is about a sense of inevitability; it's about a sense that something is happening which cannot happen otherwise. In a sense that's also one of the definitions of great art: you feel you're in the presence of great art when you feel that if any single thing was changed in this piece of work – whether it's a piece of music or a painting or a poem – if one tiny thing was changed the whole thing would collapse. It could not be otherwise than it is. The artifice, of course, is to give you that impression, I'm not saying that it's literally true, but that's what's being created, the sense that this thing that has been created is the way it is and could be no other. One of the reasons why tragedy is such a powerful form when it is created is that it comes exactly out of that sense that what happens to these people is what must happen. There is a sense of destiny, a sense of fate at work.

It is not actually possible for Mena in *Sive* to behave differently from the way she does because she is caught between incompatible desires. She actually wants to be a good person, she wants to be a happy person, she wants to be a good wife, she wants to have a nice husband, she wants to have her own children: she wants to do things which are not at all nasty or evil. At the same time in order to do that, she must involve herself in an extraordinarily sordid bargain.

Even if you look beyond a big figure like Mena there's a wonderful tiny moment in *Sive* which I think really is the mark of great theatrical writing – a figure who in other hands would be just a little cruel, mean, selfish, small man of no real import or status – the matchmaker Thomasheen, the man who is trying to do the deal and sell Sive to the old farmer. We see him for most of the play as this horrible little fixer, the worst of gombeen Ireland, who is out for what he can get and is ruining other people's lives simply in pursuit of his own selfishness. Then there's a moment in the play quite late on where Mena and Thomasheen are talking, and Mike is having second thoughts about selling Sive off and he's talking about how maybe they shouldn't do this and he says: 'The money is a great temptation but there's wrong in it from head to heel. Sive is young with a brain on her, she'll be dreaming about love with a young man; it's the way young girls do be'. And Thomasheen comes up to him and he says: 'will you listen to him? Love, in the name of God, what would the likes of us know about love?' He turns to Mena and he points a finger at Mike:

> *Did you ever hear the word of 'love' on his lips? Ah, you did not, girl. Did he ever give you a little rub behind the ear or run his fingers through your hair and tell you he would swim the Shannon for you? Did he ever sing the love songs for you in the far out part at night when ye do be alone? He would sooner to stick his snout in a plate of mate and cabbage, or rub the back of a fattening pig than whisper a bit of his fondness for you.*

And you're watching this and you are thinking, well yes of course that's what he would say, this is in his interests, he's just giving you a view of the world which actually is trying to make sure that Mena stays onside and carries through with it. Up to this point you still see him as exactly the kind of figure as you've seen him, but this goes on then and Thomasheen has a wonderful line, the most stark, bleak line – 'what I say is what business have the likes of us with love?' – and then it shifts into what I think is a tragic mode. He says:

> *What I say is what business have the likes of us with love? It is enough to have to find the bite to eat. When I was a young man twenty years ago, my father, God rest him, put a finish to my bit of love.*

And Mena says, 'You had love?'

> *I had a wish for a girl from the other side of the mountain. But what was the good when I had no place to take her? There was a frightful curam of us in my father's house with nothing but a sciath of spuds on the floor to fill us. I had two pigs fattening. My father, God rest him, was an amadawn, a stump of a fool who took his life by his own hand. He hung himself from a tree near the house. I swear to you he would never have hanged himself but he knew my two pigs would pay for his wake and funeral. 'Twas the meanness in his heart, for he knew well I had my heart set on marriage …*

And you're suddenly moved into a mythic world. That is not a sociological description – you're not in *The Sopranos* with the psychiatrist trying to understand the nasty gangster. You're in a world where Thomasheen is how he is because of a mythic act, because his father out of some kind of extraordinary spite hangs himself outside the front door because he knows that the son has gathered enough money to pay for his wedding and that that money can be used for his own funeral. It's an extraordinary moment and it is a moment of pure genius because you suddenly at that moment flip from Thomasheen being a recognisable, sociological baddie into being a genuinely tragic figure whose fate has been set by a moment that is as wild and inexplicable and strange as any moment in Greek drama.

It's a moment like Agamemnon killing his daughter so that the ships would sail. It's not a sociological moment, a moment where you think, 'well people behave like that all the time. That's a recognisable human trait, we all kill our daughters when the winds aren't coming and we need to set sail; or we all hang ourselves outside the front door when we know that our son has the money put by for his own wedding.' It's not a moment of description of typical human behaviour. It's a moment out of myth and when it interrupts you, it has an extraordinary effect in the theatre. When it's done well you are as a person watching it in two frames at the same time: you're watching the unfolding of a credible story about 1950s Ireland and about people about whom you can understand why they behave the way they behave. Then you're flipped into this sudden shift where you are in a world that is absolutely timeless and is absolutely universal and grotesque. And it comes out of nowhere and it is inexplicable: you can't understand why someone hangs himself outside the door to spite his son's marriage. It's a biblical moment, it's a mythical moment, and it's a moment rising from a deep sense of the way in which human lives are shaped by the grotesque and the awful. At that moment, Thomasheen actually becomes almost a sort of heroic figure. He becomes somebody who has the burden of something extraordinary placed on his shoulders and he's behaving the way he is now not just because he's a grubby little fool who wants to meddle in people's lives and get some advantage out of it but because he has something like the curse of Cain on him. He has this thing imprinted on his soul which again comes up almost, as it were, out of nowhere, out of something that we cannot explain or put our fingers on.

The ability to do that, which he does at moments in those great plays, is something that puts Keane in very high company indeed. There aren't many writers, in the English language in the theatre in the twentieth century, who have that capacity to shift our consciousness at certain moments on the stage and to make us feel that extraordinary tension that you get very rarely with even very powerful theatre when you feel like you've ceased just to be yourself sitting in a recognisable theatre with recognisable people with recognisable problems and are suddenly brought up against the fact that we exist in a universe that is rational up to a point and beyond that is absurd and inexplicable. It's a moment that you get sometimes in Beckett, that you get sometimes in Pinter, you get sometimes in Sam Sheppard's plays, you get sometimes in Tom Murphy's plays, in Brian Friel's plays. The fact that you get it in Keane's plays demands of us that we look at that work again in ways which try to respect its richness and the extraordinary imagination that was capable of bringing those two world views, those two time-frames to bear on the situation of a small and relatively ordinary society on the western edge of Europe in the late 1950s.

A Portrait of the Artist as an Emerging Playwright

Nóra Relihan

John B. Keane, known in his younger days simply as 'John Keane', began writing as a schoolboy. His education began in Listowel Boys' National School where, through one of those strange quirks of fate, one of his teachers was Bryan Mac-Mahon, an already well-known Listowel writer, and from the same street – Church Street! John B. immortalised the street in his now famous poem, 'The Street', which was to become the title poem of his poetry collection. I can see him now of an evening – many an evening – holding court in his pub, eyes closed, reciting what was to become a hallmark of his party pieces. He requested that I would learn it also and include it in my solo shows. I did indeed often recite 'The Street' (see p. 79) when on tour – and of course on radio and television.

Growing up in Listowel, a small, rural town that is – architecturally at least – typical of many such in southern Ireland, brought with it much to observe for the budding writer.

The fine Norman square bore prominent witness to both God and Mammon, with the predominant religions, Roman Catholic and Church of Ireland, bearing witness in two impressive churches, while Mammon proudly prospered in the square's three finest buildings which housed branches of the three major Irish banks. Doctors, dentists, lawyers, other professional practitioners, traders, a commercial hotel and a variety of private citizens gave the square its stamp.

The rest of the town had the usual mix of shopkeepers, craftspeople and artisans typical of most small towns of the time in rural Ireland. Outdoor pursuits included Gaelic football – in which John B. took an active interest – handball, camogie and a tennis club with the big festival of Listowel Races providing a perennial highlight. Greyhound breeding, training and racing were also taking a big hold on rural Ireland. And, of course, the town's much loved water feature, the Feale River, was a source of endless diversion.

Amateur drama was a big indoor hobby during the winter months – often touring play companies and fit-up variety shows came to perform; even the celebrated actor/manager, Anew McMaster, brought his unique and flamboyant productions of Shakespeare's more famous plays to Listowel. Indeed his own portrayal of Othello is still remembered. St Patrick's Hall in Patrick Street – or 'William Street' – housed a bridge club and billiards (for men), also a brass band and a busy musical society.

So, it was into this pleasant and peaceful town that John Brendan Keane was born on 21 July 1928. His siblings included five boys and four girls. Growing up under the influence of his teacher-father, Bill – who could even boast of having a library in the house – and his mother, Hannah Purtill, a Cumann na mBan veteran, he had a secure childhood. But, apart from all the permeating influences of home and town, an even more exciting and almost magical atmosphere captured his young imagination. He had country cousins in the nearby Stacks Mountains. It became his favourite place and he spent his school holidays there – indeed, his mother was to say that she could get him to come home only with difficulty! It was here that he heard tales of matchmaking and superstitions, of heroes and heroines of the Fianna, of great deeds and mean deeds. And, of course, his lifelong fascination with matchmaking began here, dominated by the image of one famous practitioner of the 'art' – Dan Paddy Andy.

I would like to quote from one of a recent series I wrote for Lyric FM to describe my first meeting with John B.: 'Two figures emerge from memory's mist from a 1950s hospital setting – a young woman in a nurse's uniform and a tall, thin, dark-haired young man riding a bicycle to the entrance of

Listowel Hospital. He carried an apothecary's valise containing replenishments for the hospital medicine cupboard.'

I was a young nurse, back from London and recently qualified. The young man introduced himself as 'John Keane'; he worked as an assistant to a local chemist, Mr William Keane-Stack – now long deceased. He turned out to be a rather unusual chemist's assistant. On his next visit, not alone did he bring the required medicines but, as we sorted through the hospital requirements, he hesitantly removed a few folded sheets of paper from the inside pocket of his jacket and proffered them to me: 'Would you ever take a look at this couple of short stories I've written? – I'm thinking of sending them off to the *Evening Press*'.

Having been interested in theatre since childhood, I had become actively involved with Listowel Drama Group which had been founded some years before by Eamonn Kelly and Bryan MacMahon. It was then the only drama group in Listowel and had built up a very good reputation through competing on the Drama Festival circuit. In 1958, John B. saw my prize-winning production of Joseph Tomelty's play, *All Souls' Night*. Shortly after, during a chance encounter on the street, he informed me that he was not greatly impressed by Tomelty's play and was going to write a play himself.

By now, John was married to Mary O'Connor from Knocknagoshel and they were living in their recently acquired public house in William Street. It was here, in the back-kitchen, that *Sive* was created in three or four weeks in what must have been a near-frenzied spell of continuous writing – much of it throughout the night.

John then presented the play to the management of the Abbey Theatre who rejected it apparently without comment. He then approached Listowel Drama Group through their secretary, Bill Kearney. Bill, who was later to give a memorable performance as Thomasheen Seán Rua, the matchmaker, took an instant liking to the play. Consultation with Micheál Ó hAodha followed – he was head of drama in Radio Éireann – and he supported Bill's view. A decision was quickly taken – *Sive*, directed by Brendan Carroll, would be our next production.

There is a traditional saying in Listowel that 'nothing happens until after the Races' – that is the big annual race meeting held at the end of September. The casting of *Sive* did not begin until the autumn of 1958. At that time, and for many years later, 'getting a part in a play' was regarded as quite an achievement. In a financially depressed climate, disposable income was very limited, putting many hobbies out of bounds for the average earner – the Celtic Tiger was not even a gleam in the nation's eye! Hence, a relatively inexpensive hobby like amateur drama continued to flourish. Indeed, stage presentations generally did well during Lent. Laws of both church and state demanded that no dances be held during the penitential season under pain of all manner of unmentionable punishments. 'Close dancing' was preached about with something like horror at Sunday masses and during the parish mission when threatening 'fire and brimstone' from the pulpit was the order of the day.

There was great demand for parts in the drama group. The casting sessions were tense and exciting. At least three people were auditioned for each part. Readings continued over three or four evenings and for several hours each evening – pub closing time usually dictated our stopping time! Sometimes a likely-looking actor-in-the-making from outside the group was coaxed in to face what was quite an ordeal – to be auditioned in front of a half dozen or so 'experts'! Indeed Margaret Dillon, now Margaret Ward, who played Sive, was herself hauled in from the classroom.

In 1958, casting completed, it was decided to take rehearsals to the old Protestant school in the square. A workshop atmosphere prevailed during the rehearsals, with John B. nearly always in attendance. The sessions were a great learning experience. Looking back, it was wonderful to have the writer, the actors and the director exchanging views on dialogue, movement and characterisation. And if memory serves me right, almost to a man and a woman, we smoked like chimneys! One exception, of course, was the lovely Sive. Margaret would be found in a quiet corner doing her homework when not required on the set.

Memories of those first rehearsals, although fragmentary, are still vivid. Playing juvenile leads had been my lot in previous productions and now, cast as the bitter, childless Mena Glavin, I was suddenly thrust into my first character part. 'Married' to Mike Glavin, a part which Kevin O'Donovan made his own, I had to contend with his stage mother at close quarters – Nanna Glavin, played wonderfully by my late dear friend, Siobhán Cahill. The Nanna/Mena scenes were filled with open jealousies, resentments and suspicions. Off stage, we were such good friends, while, in character, 'two lightin' divils' would describe us!

My memory of the initial impact of the sound of John B.'s dramatic language is etched deep. Elizabethan words mixed with Hiberno-English, dotted with insults, humour and 'strong' language sometimes caused even the cast to draw in breath during the early days of rehearsal. My first sighting of Hilary Neilson in the character of Seán Dota, the awful old man whom Sive was being forced to marry, made me want to laugh and cry all at the one time. Other unforgettable moments from those 1958 rehearsals remain: the first sight and sound of John Cahill as Carthalawn singing 'Oh Mike Glavin you're the man' to his own accompaniment on the bodhrán – described at that time in the script as a 'tambourine'. And John Flaherty – Carthalawn's father, Pats Bocock – limping in beside him carrying his dangerous-looking blackthorn stick which he used to direct the drum-beat and to point at the next unfortunate victim of Carthalawn's verse.

About half-way through the rehearsals of any play, a scene here or there starts to really come together. One evening in the shadowy light permeating the old stone building, we were 'polishing' the final scene of the play. Liam Scuab, Sive's boyfriend, brought in her dead, drowned body. Mike, accompanied by the matchmaker, went for the priest. Seán Dota slipped away. Liam stood by the table which I cleared, delph and all, in one movement on the floor. He laid Sive on the table, sobbing as he gently dried her hair. Then Liam Scuab, played by that wonderful actor, Brian Brennan, turned to Mena – me. His words hissed through the air like bullets: 'You killed her! You! You horrible filthy bitch! That the hand of Jesus might strike you dead where you stand!' I was genuinely riveted to the spot!

Sive opened on 2 February 1959 at Walshe's Super Ballroom, Listowel, to an astonished audience who laughed, cried and pronounced themselves both 'delighted' and 'shocked' by 'the language'. Packed houses ensued. Drama festivals were won and one memorable one was lost. The All Ireland Drama Festival's Esso Trophy fell thrall to *Sive*'s magic. We played the Abbey Theatre in May when Ernest Blythe expressed interest in my joining the company – a husband and small daughter in Listowel took precedence! The Wexford Opera Festival invited us for October. Margaret and I 'guested' with the Southern Theatre Group in Cork during that summer of 1959. Then I played the Grand Opera House, Belfast, Dublin's Olympia Theatre a few times, and much more. *Sive* drew packed houses everywhere.

John B. and I founded the Listowel Players. Micheál Ó hAodha produced the LP of *Sive* with the Listowel Players at the Leo Whelan studio in Dublin. A good many of the original cast played their same parts, with John B. himself as Pats Bocock and his brother Eamonn as Mike Glavin.

I have always believed that John B. Keane will be remembered for being a superb folk-dramatist who has saved a precious idiom from possible extinction, and who had the talent to put that idiom into the mouths of never-to-be forgotten characters!

Common Themes in John B. Keane and Brendan Kennelly

Paddy McElligott and Pat Moore

On the road from Listowel to Tarbert (the N69) in the summer of 2003, a landowner set about reclaiming bogland. In the process he uncovered what looks like North Kerry's oldest forest. The roots of 5,000-year-old woodland became visible, sitting there like giant sculptures bearing witness to the landscape's story from some time after the ice age. This bogland was once part of a huge forest that covered a sizable part of North Kerry, from Ballyheigue over to Graffa and on to West Limerick. Maybe no human being ever walked these forests, but the forests were there, silent; shaping the landscape we try to shape. In fact, that landscape has shaped us.

In the same way, both John B. Keane and Brendan Kennelly have uncovered the subconscious in North Kerry as they dealt in many of their writings with birth, death, and all the issues that come before and after. To begin, let Moloney be introduced. He is a character Kennelly moulded from the North Kerry lore, camaraderie and traditions with which he grew up:

Moloney Remembers the Resurrection of Kate

Finucane

O she was a handsome corpse, he said,
Divil a difference between livin' and dead
You'd see in her; a fine red face
On a starchy pillow edged with lace,
Her cold hands clasped, her mousy hair
As neatly tied as a girl's at a fair.
Touchin' forty she was when she passed away,
But twenty she looked as she lay
In bed on the broad of her back.
Kate Finucane of Asdee West
Was stretched in death, but she looked her best!

Her cousins had come
From all parts of the Kingdom
For the wake; Coffeys and Lanes from Dingle,
McCarthys and Ryans, married and single,
Honest and otherwise. For a day and a night
As she lay in her bed, a sight
For sore eyes, they drank and they prayed
And they sang her to heaven – as fine
A wake as ever I went to in all my time!

Well, there was nothin' to do, after prayin' and drinkin',
But lift herself into the coffin.
'Twas at that moment, glory to God,
As I stood with my glass at the head
Of her bed, that she stretched like a cat and opened her eyes
And lifted her head in great surprise;
And motherogod will I ever forget
The cut an' the go, the sight an' the set
Of her when, calm as you like, with a toss of her head,
Kate Finucane sat up in the bed!

No need to tell
Of all the commotion that fell
On the cousins, neighbours, myself and the house.

Dead she'd been, and now this disastrous
Return to life, upsettin' the whole
Place, and I thinkin' her body was lackin' a soul.
But after a while, things quietened down
And Kate made tea for the cousins. She found
She'd not seen them for ages. What's more,
She clapped her eyes on a Lenamore
Man called Harty, and three months later,
Paraded him in rare style up to the altar!
On top o' that, she showed the world she could
Make a dandy wife, for she's still to the good,
And without doubt of favour, fright or fear,
Kate Finucane has a child a year!

Gay woman, Kate, Moloney said
Divil a difference between livin' and dead!

Both writers draw from the same well of time and landscape where words, imagination, story and humour are used to honour human experience. In Keane, the countryside was allowed to speak through him as the musty damp places often gave way to soaring insights into humanity. We find examples in *The Field* and *Sive*. The next piece is the song about the young girl Sive:

THE SIVE SONG

Oh, come all good men and true, a sad tale I'll tell to you
Of a maiden who was known to me as Sive.
She was young and sweet and fair but that household sad and bare
Her marriage to an old man would contrive.

Now the Tinker's son came in to that house of want and sin

And his father Pats Bocock smote on the floor
Saying 'Carthalawn, my blade, let a noble song be made
Bringing plenty on this house for evermore.'

Oh Mike Glavin, you're the man; you was always in the van
With an open door to oul' man and gorsoon
May white snuff be at your wake, baker's bread and curran-y cake
And the plenty on your table late and soon.

But they scorned the Tinker's son when his song of praise was done
And his father Pats Bocock smote on the floor
Saying 'Carthalawn, my jewel, let a song both wild and cruel
Settle down upon this house for evermore.'

On the road from Abbeyfeale, sure I met a man with meal
Come here says he and pass your idle time;
On me he made quite bold, saying the young will wed the old
And the old man have the money for the child.

Now Thomasheen Rua, the liar, was sat down 'longside the fire
And he sold the girl Sive that very night
Pats Bocock made on his quest, saying, 'sing your mighty best.'
And the song of Carthalawn was like a blight.

May the snails devour his corpse, and the rains do harm worse,
May the devil sweep the hairy creature soon,
He's as greedy as a sow, as a crow behind the plough
The black man from the mountain, Seánín Rua.

May he screech with awful thirst, may his brains and eyeballs burst,
That melted amadán, that big bostoon.
May the fleas ate up his bed, and the mange consume his head
The black man from the mountain, Seánín Rua.

But the Bonny Sive took flight, like a wild bird in the night
And the waters washed her small white body o'er
And her true love found her there, and he stacked her golden hair
And he laid her on the dark and dismal shore.

Then outspoke bold Pats Bocock and his voice was sad with shock,
And his face was grey as winter when he cried.
He said, 'Carthalawn, my gem, let you make a woeful hymn
All of this day and of the one who died.'

Oh, come all good men and true, a sad tale I'll tell to you
All of a maiden fair who died this day.
Oh, they drownded lovely Sive, for she would not be a bride
And they laid her dead to bury in the clay.

Both men had football and the pub in common. This meant that they were meeting people on a daily basis. It developed a sympathetic nature in them, which meant that both women and men found it easy to confide in them. People told them their stories feeling that this could be added to the contribution the authors themselves were making to our understanding of ourselves.

Story is the first place we see this interaction. John B. Keane can make the ordinary extraordinary through a story line in a play but also in a short story. The following piece is one of his short stories, adapted for storytelling (by Paddy McElligott):

YOU'RE ON NEXT SUNDAY

The 15 August in the year of Our Lord 1934 – it was a fair year for primroses, a better one for hay, and a woeful year for funerals!
My grandfather Muirisheen Connor tackled the pony, called for his auld friend Thady Dowd of Lacca, and headed for Ballybunion for the fifteenth. That was their lifelong pattern on Pattern Day. He wouldn't take me – I was too young at the time.

Their first stop was into Mikey-Joe's, the Americano Bar for a pint and a stiff one inside in it to keep it company. They trailed pub to pub and after a solid day's drinking, they were ousted by the Civic Guard, but not before investing in a noggin of whiskey apiece to shorten the road home.

They were going at a nice jogtrot in the pony and trap when all of a slap the pony stopped dead in his tracks beside Gale graveyard and no amount of coaxing would move him a single solitary inch. There was an eerie silence – 'I don't like the look of it,' says my grand-father and he starts a quick Hail Mary for the dead. The pony was frothing at the mouth, with a look of abject terror in his bloodshot eyes, terrible to behold.

Dowd took another slug out of the noggin and says, 'I don't give a rattling damn,' as he hopped down out of the trap. He leaned in over the graveyard gate and let this béic out of him – anam 'on dia-bhal – before him were two hurling teams, dressed in togs, shorts and slippers – a camán in every hand. 'What's the matter?' shouts Dowd. A tall player with a face as white as limestone came over to him and says, 'I'm the captain and we're short a man.' 'Who are the teams?' says Dowd. 'We're Ballyduff and the others are Ballybawn,' says the captain. 'Ho-ho,' says Thady, 'I'm your man. My mother, God be good to her, was a Ballyduff woman!' The captain agreed and Thady climbed over the gate.

The pitch, which was the length and breadth of the graveyard, lit up and forms appeared from the ground and sat on the graveyard wall. A bald ref in a white shirt blew an ancient hunting horn and threw in the sliotar. Ballybawn was the faster outfit and for a while it was like snowballs coming into the Ballyduff square. Dowd was taking no prisoners and after a while the ref cautioned him for abu-sive language and dirty play in general. A skirmish broke out in the crowd near the gate and a cocoa canister was thrown at the ref – he threatened to call off the game if they didn't behave.

Half time came and went and both teams were giving it every-thing. My grandfather said that the hurling was as good as he had ever seen, with lovely wristwork and pulling, and fine long-range points.

Five minutes to go and the teams were level. The ghostly forms jumped up and down on the walls. One minute to go and a melee broke out in mid-field – you could hear the clash of the ash on doughty skulls. Dowd won possession and with a savage drunken yell he cut through the Ballybawn players like a scythe through switch-grass, the ball poised on the base of his hurley – he darts like a trout – he bounds like a stag. He leaped over grave mounds with the entire Ballybawn team on his heels like a pack of hungry hounds. He skirted crosses at breakneck speed and was upended onto a tombstone. The ref blew his horn for a free.

There was liquid flowing down along the side of Dowd's leg; his first thought was for the noggin of whiskey. He put his hand down; ''Tis all right,' says he, ''tis only blood!' He finished the noggin and squared up for the free. He rolled the sliotar on to his camán and lashed at it. It went away to the right, passed through the eye of a Celtic cross; it rebounded off the poll of a plaster angel and was directed towards the goals by the extended hand of the figure of Michael the Archangel. It skeeved inside the left upright and found its way to the back of the net: CÚL!

The crowd went wild. Dowd had got Ballyduff into the next round of the West Munster Graveyard Cup. He was lifted aloft and trotted 'round the graveyard and given three cheers. Hip-hip … hip-hip … hip-hip …

Three eerie ullagones went heavenwards and died slowly. The teams and crowd vanished save for the Ballyduff captain. 'Come on quick,' says my grandfather. Just as Dowd was about to clear the gate the captain placed a ghostly hand firmly on his right shoulder; 'You played a star,' says he. 'You're the pride of your mother's people. Go home and get your affairs in order. You're on for good next Sunday.'

Didn't I tell you it was a woeful year for funerals!

Many of John B.'s short stories capture a different era to the one that today's students are growing up in. They expose the young scholar to a sense of life at that time and, with a good dollop of John B.'s humour, they develop an appreciation of life in North Kerry before cars, before annual holidays, before television, when storytelling and personal interaction were the most common form of diversion and entertainment. Many of his short stories over the years were published in *The Limerick Leader*. Brendan Kennelly could reflect on the power the story has in our lives, holding things together, and he sees the danger inherent in losing our story or losing a story that gelled us together. His poem, 'The Story', clearly defines his thinking on this:

THE STORY

The story was not born with Robbie Cox
Nor with his father
Nor with his father's father
But farther back than any could remember.

Cox told the story
Over twelve nights of Christmas.
It was the story
Made Christmas real.
When it was done
The new year was in,
Made authentic by the story.
The old year was dead,
Buried by the story.
The man endured,
Deepened by the story.

When Cox died
The story died.
Nobody had time
To learn the story.
Christmas shrivelled.
The old year was dust,
The new year nothing special,
So much time to be endured.

The people withered.
This withering hardly troubled them.
The story was a dead crow in a wet field,
An abandoned house, a rag on a bush,
A sick whisper in a dying room,
The shaking gash of an old man's mouth
Breaking like burnt paper
Into black ashes the wind scatters,
People fleeing from famine.
Nobody has ever heard of them.
Nobody will ever speak for them.
I know the emptiness
Spread by the story's death.
This emptiness is in the roads
And in the fields,
In men's eyes and children's voices,
In summer nights when stars
Play like rabbits behind Cox's house,
House of the story
That once lived on lips
Like starlings startled from a tree,
Exploding in a sky of revelation,
Deliberate and free.

Both men sense that in rural Ireland we may have fallen out of our story – lost the plot through amnesia, yet they don't waste time on moralising. They see that the best criticism of the bad is the practice of the better, and by telling their stories well they honour what is best in us.

Land and history are linked and form the basis for both writers' most significant contributions. Kennelly's poem 'My Dark Fathers' first published in 1964 gives us the reason for the hold the land has on us. It stretches back to the famine, it is in our subconscious and it is formative of our behaviour:

My Dark Fathers

My dark fathers lived the intolerable day
Committed always to the night of wrong,
Stiffened at the hearthstone, the woman lay,
Perished feet nailed to her man's breastbone.
Grim houses beckoned in the swelling gloom
Of Munster fields where the Atlantic night
Fettered the child within the pit of doom,
And everywhere a going down of light.

And yet upon the sandy Kerry shore
The woman once had danced at ebbing tide
Because she loved flute music – and still more
Because a lady wondered at the pride
Of one so humble. That was long before
The green plant withered by an evil chance;
When winds of hunger howled at every door
She heard the music dwindle and forgot the dance.

Such mercy as the wolf receives was hers
Whose dance became a rhythm in a grave,
Achieved beneath the thorny savage furze
That yellowed fiercely in a mountain cave.
Immune to pity, she, whose crime was love,
Crouched, shivered, searched the threatening sky,
Discovered ready signs, compelled to move
Her to her innocent appalling cry.

Skeletoned in darkness, my dark fathers lay
Unknown, and could not understand
The giant grief that trampled night and day,
The awful absence moping through the land.
Upon the headland, the encroaching sea
Left sand that hardened after tides of spring,
No dancing feet disturbed its symmetry
And those who loved good music ceased to sing.

> *Since every moment of the clock*
> *Accumulates to form a final name,*
> *Since I am come of Kerry clay and rock,*
> *I celebrate the darkness and the shame*
> *That could compel a man to turn his face*
> *Against the wall, withdrawn from light so strong*
> *And undeceiving, spancelled in a place*
> *Of unapplauding hands and broken song.*

Indeed, its image of a husband and wife lying dead, he having placed her feet inside the neck of his shirt to give her his last vestiges of body heat, imprint the picture of despair and oppression in the student's mind in a more powerful way than any history textbook.

The Bull McCabe knows the importance of our relationship with land in *The Field*, and he knows it when he looks at a field springing to life in the month of April. We ignore this bond in us at our peril. Keane had an intimate understanding of this binding that is inherent in our heritage. His love of his own home place is evident in this poem about Listowel that he wrote as a teenager:

THE STREET

> *I love the flags that pave the walk.*
> *I love the mud between,*
> *The funny figures drawn in chalk.*
> *I love to hear the sound*
> *Of drays upon their round,*
> *Of horses and their clock-like walk.*

I love to watch the corner-people gawk
And hear what underlies their idle talk.

I love to hear the music of the rain.
I love to hear the sound
Of yellow waters flushing in the main.
I love the breaks between
When little boys begin
To sail their paper galleons in the drain.
Grey clouds sail west and silver-tips remain.
The street, thank God, is bright and clean again.

Here, within a single street,
Is everything that is,
Of pomp and blessed poverty made sweet
And all that is of love
Of man and God above.
Of happiness and sorrow and conceit,
Of tragedy and death and bitter-sweet,
Of hope, despair, illusion and defeat.

A golden mellow peace forever clings
Along the little street.
There are so very many lasting things
Beyond the wall of strife
In our beleaguered life.
There are so many lovely songs to sing
Of God and His eternal love that rings
Of simple people and of simple things.

Kennelly shows us that intrigue, ill-will and greed are erupting in our modern, urban, media-driven world; for the human soul never fails to wander on exploring its heights and depths wherever it finds itself. Death and love are biblical themes. They are themes in world literature and it is on these huge rites of passage that both writers hang many of their insightful perspectives and plots. Death as a reality is never avoided. It is humoured, ducked, mocked, but never avoided. It is given the final say of respect:

MOLONEY AT THE WAKE

That was a gay night, he said,
I went to a wake and hopped into bed
With the corpse; not a very nice
Thing to do, I suppose; cold as ice
Her belly and thighs;
Two brown pennies covered her eyes;
They'd tied up her foxy hair
And crossed her hands as though in prayer.
When alive, the same girl wasn't much
Given to prayers and such,
But they made her look as though she could
Have prayed the legs from under God.
Anyway, I got into bed
There and then beside the dead
Woman; a disastrous
Thing to do because the whole house
Thought I was mad. I drew a long
Breath, looked at her and broke into song.
With her icy belly against my knee
I sang 'Old girl, why don't you answer me?'
Christ, man, talk of a scatter! The whole place
Panicked; 'tis a terrible disgrace,
They said, when a drunken sot the like o' you
Can stagger in here through
The open door, and without an attempt at a prayer
Make a wild buck-lepp in there
Beside herself, and she stretched.
Never mind, I said,
What do you, or I, know of the dead?
Of course, I grant that politeness must be shown
At all times, so I'll get up now and leave her alone.

Two mugs o' porter, a quick Hail Mary for the dead,
Then I hit for home and the wife in bed.
I was glad to see her, she to see me,
We were both as livin' as we needed to be
To do as our bodies prayed us to do.
When the soul is a liar, the body is true.
A body is all a poor man has got
And love is a moment before we rot.
Moloney smiled and lifted his glass:
"Tis a privilege to drink to all things that pass.'

Neither is the reality of love avoided. It too is humoured, ducked and mocked yet it is celebrated more by its absence than its presence. There is a sense in the work of Keane that love is joy yet to come – or indeed lust that may never come!

Extract from LETTERS OF A MATCHMAKER

> Coolkera
> Coomasahara

Dear Mr O'Connor,
I tried your recipe and went back to Mickeen Snoss. He was with the doctor and he was told there was no cure for his ailment and 'tis me that knows it for didn't I give the past three weeks under the one quilt with him. I'd be better engaged sleeping with a corpse. Now like a good man will you forward my money by return of post.

> *Fionnuala Crust (Miss)*

> Spiders' Well
> Ballybara

Dear Mrs Snoss,
Am I supposed to go around like a veterinary surgeon examining and inspecting candidates or like a department man passing bulls.

Did you try poitcheen on him internal and external? You're not doing your job right. Isn't it well known that doctors have no cure for what ails Mickeen. If they had they'd be millionaires. You'd be better off going to a nurse or a chemist's shop.

There is pills. There is bottles and lotions. There is blisters and whatnot there for taking that would improve his condition. Where there's life there's hope. There's roundy yokes called oysters that is swallowed alive out of their shells and what fills men with taspy what was only fit for the grave before. The poitcheen is your handiest remedy of all. I remember Nell Tobin's turkey cock Patsy what she used to stand on market days at the back of Emery's pub. After servicing three hens in a row the cock would be inclined to fall back and stagger and there would come a glassy look into his eyes. From under her shawl Nell would bring a black bottle. Inside would be a half-pint of poitcheen. She'd throw the cock on the flat of his back and pour a crawful down his piobawn. She'd follow this with a pill and in five minutes the cock would be anxious for more hens. If turkey cocks can be got going with pills and poitcheen why not old men?

Lamp oil or petrol rubbed into the backbone is another good way and there is them what swears by a turpentine blister applied to the afflicted area. Another way is coaxiorum. There is nine different ways of using this but two is all I know. One is to prick holes in an orange and put it between your breasts for two days and then give it to him to eat. By all accounts there will be no ram or no boar or no puck the bate of him after this. Another way is to fire a grain of your water on the back of his pole and he asleep. There is reported to be seven other ways and if there is any old woman handy she may know a few. Don't write to me no more letters now like a good woman but go back to your lawfully wedded husband and apply yourself to the job you were armed for.

Civility and courtesy assured at all times.

Your obt. servant
Dicky Mick Dicky O'Connor

There is a whiff off Kennelly's work that love is joy that has been experienced:

BATTERED

He sits in his battered Ford in the dark
outside his home. For hours. Why
won't he go in?
His wife has just given birth,
the stones are sniggering.
'Who's the father of the lad?' they ask.

The battered Ford accommodates a man
at home only in the dark
and blinding hours of work.

Kennelly inhabits a landscape brought to light by his poetic eye, which gives him the ability to see life grilled down to the essentials; for the poet is a wordsmith.

The sense of what is, and was, and what is to come, gives both writers a sense of the transient. God is real and present. The language of Keane can be legalistic judgement accompanied by an intuitive grasp of human nature. Kennelly speaks a sacramental language that goes towards the light.

Every region has its share of writers, but North Kerry has been blessed with numerous other great writers: Maurice Walsh, George Fitzmaurice, Bryan MacMahon and Gabriel Fitzmaurice to name but a few. It is no exaggeration to suggest that their presence was never as significant, given the chaotic rate of cultural and social change during these times in which we live. While the change is to be welcomed and embraced, bedlam could result unless we are fully aware of the cultural road we have travelled to get to where we are. In this respect, the perception and compassion of the local writer can be a cornerstone for young students as they are shaped by their fast-moving world.

The local writer has so much to offer to the student. This is identified in the language used, the similarity in interpretation. In this context, the local student has a substantial advantage over highly qualified scholars who have not experienced the same local nuances and linguistic evolution. The students in the area have drunk from the same well, know where to find the good bushes for red-berried holly, and have built castles with the same sand. Given the advantages bestowed on the students simply by the circumstances of their birth, it is disingenuous not to introduce them to others who have stripped away the trimmings of their surroundings and have exposed the roots – the roots that have nourished us and shaped us into what we are.

John B. Keane, Society, Country, Culture and Language: The Lonely Heart

Michael Scott

My relationship with John B. goes back to about 1989 when I was talking to Phyllis Ryan who has in fact produced, as you probably all know, a huge number of John B.'s plays. She had taken risks with John's plays when nobody else would do it, and presented them all over the place. She said to me, 'I've got this little-known play, we haven't done it for years and it's really good: it's called *The Matchmaker* – it'd do really well'. I was at the time running the Tivoli Theatre in Dublin and we were looking for a new show. So I said, 'fine, whatever it is – how many in it?'

'Two.'

I was busy preparing for another production, so I didn't direct it: Phyllis put it together and I ended up doing the now famous publicity photograph of Anna Manahan and Frank Kelly. We put it on initially for two weeks and it completely sold out for us.

Before we mounted the production, I'd never met John B. and so we all went to Listowel on a 'field-trip' because we decided we were going to have John B. make a ' voice over' at the beginning of the show. I met John in his pub and we ended up having a long walk together along the beach at Ballybunion and telling each other funny stories. (Later that day I went off to various houses to find tape-recorders that were working so that I could record John B.) It was a magical sort of experience, an experience that I never forgot. And in retrospect it's an experience where I met 'John the Poet', because as I came to realise later when I got to know him better, you couldn't know John without realising that he spoke in prose and poetry. It wasn't something he sat down and had work at to do – when he spoke, he spoke either prose or poetry, quite naturally. Sometimes he'd take a diversion and make it a poetic moment but generally, the language he used himself was a poetic language.

The year before he died, we were doing the video of *The Matchmaker* and I decided we'd take a video of John in the pub doing the same introduction on video that he did for the play voice-over. He was very sick: ten years beforehand when we'd done it he'd been able to do it in a blink; however long it took to read it, that's how long he took to do it. When we went down to do the video bit he was so nervous (because he was so sick) – and none of us at that time thought he was dying. John thought he was dying but nobody would believe it – but it took us hours to do what is effectively two minutes fourteen seconds and we had to make twelve cuts because all John could get to do was to say: 'Dicky Mick Dicky resides in Spiderwell, Ballybarra ...' and we had to cut it all the time because he was so petrified and so upset. I said to him eventually, 'John, the one thing I have to have from you is ... will you just relax? Because it's when you look at the camera and you talk, your warmth – it's that storyteller in you that the audience want to see.' This is what you get in all of the plays: John was a storyteller. His ability as a human being, his own natural ability floods the work. I can hardly ever think of any piece of John's writing, without hearing how John would have wanted the tone, the rhythm, the sound and the punctuation, to be.

John was in a terrible state and I said to him, 'would you do an interview with me because these people want me to do an interview with you? Why don't I just put the video camera on and ask you a few questions?' And I think he did a half hour interview – having taken two hours to do two minutes twelve seconds – he did a half hour interview in twenty-nine and a half minutes, because, once he was relaxed about talking, he was amazing. One of the things he spoke about was the language of the plays, that the language is a compound: it's Irish-English, it's from the Stacks Mountains, it's from

Lyreacrompane, it's the language of the people who spoke Irish and then learned English: the verbs are in the wrong place, the way of expressing is not the way you express in English. And when you get the rhythm of that correct, it unlocks the magic.

Just let me quote you something from *Sharon's Grave*, as it is an extraordinary piece of writing. Pat Spode, the pedlar, talking at the end of the play to the childless couple who got together, says:

> After you're wedded wait for news of a sickle moon in the sky. Ye must have the same soft will to ye for love. She must have a two o' wet lips and all of a softness to her. Go with her out of her warm bed at the first light of a day. Let ye be fond companions in the new light. Put you something woollen around her for airly cold. Lie her down on dewy ground with the soft wool to warm her. Face her then to the first foot's fall of a flowing tide and then let ye throw all thoughts of worries and woes away from ye. There must be a tide and ye must face the tide, a young silver tide with giddy antics. And I'll be calling within the space of a year maybe to cure a blockin' of wind in a young thing or to give advice about nursin', the Blessings of God attend ye.

It's special because it's poetic: go find the silver moon, and go make love with the tide. It's an amazing moment, but the language is extraordinary – 'a giddy tide'. People have under-estimated John's craft and his ability with words. They have for years not recognised that John's choice to write in a language he knew wasn't a choice about staying parochial, but was in fact a particular way of opening a universality for his plays. Why do the plays work for the people? Because they touch people in a language that people understand intimately and intuitively. They don't have to work at it, and people understand the plays without having to think about how they understand them: they touch them in places that they recognise from their own pasts, from their parents, from their own memories. That is one of the powers of John's creativity: instead of writing these great extraordinary 'whatevers', he stuck to what he knew and fashioned it, because he was an extraordinarily crafted writer. When, as a director, you work with his text you realise how much effort he put into the paragraph. He could sense how the character might speak: when you look at *Sharon's Grave* the language is one thing; a rural language but when you look at a play like the *The Crazy Wall* the language is different, more domestic: because he wrote in the idiom of the people who needed to speak. When he's writing *The Matchmaker* he's writing one way, when he's writing *The Field* the people are different: the way that William Dee in *The Field* speaks is completely different to the way the Bull or Mick Flanagan speaks, they make different types of sentences. That's not an accident: it's the sign of an extraordinarily good, crafted writer because he knew how the measure of the language of those characters worked. John understood how intimately character and language are interlinked.

I was very conscious that the key to John's plays – one of them – getting them to work for the audience, is that the language is elusive. It seems to be extremely simple but it's extraordinarily crafted and very, very dense. A lot of amateur companies, because they have natural accents, when they speak the language, find the rhythm of it naturally. When people try to put on the accent, they actually kill the free-flowing beauty of the language. We produced *The Matchmaker* in Dublin, then we took it to Tralee and about a week later we presented it in Donegal. They didn't laugh in Donegal for the first evening. I had neighbours in Donegal (because I have a house there), and I asked them, 'did you like it?' They said, 'well, yes, but we couldn't understand the beginning of it.' One of the things that was extraordinary was that because we'd all been down in Tralee for a week, we were all speaking naturally again within the correct rhythm; but when we went back up to Donegal – which is more than a 100 miles north – they couldn't understand the rhythm. I had to sit down and say to Des and Anna, 'you have to go back to doing it as if you're playing it in America: flatten it' – because they actually don't catch the natural rhythm of it. In Tralee everyone's going, 'oh, wow, the acting's perfect!' but in Donegal, they didn't understand it. That was interesting and we were conscious then when we took the show to Edinburgh that again we had to be careful with the language.

For Edinburgh, I got John to compose a glossary which we put in the programme – how do you explain to someone in Edinburgh: 'a lifeless latchicho …'? What does that mean? Or a 'gluchán', or whatever … And John spoke his translations off the top of his head, sometimes very racy things and said, 'you can't put that down!' and I said, 'John, you've said it, I've typed it, it's going in.' His worst one was: 'not enough of a penis for a decent wrinkle' and he said, 'You can't put that down!' and I said, 'You've said it, it's colloquial, it's going in.'

In Edinburgh, they laughed slightly more than the audiences here. In Ireland, we laugh at *The Matchmaker* because we recognise the character types, but they also recognise them in Scotland. When we took it to America, off-Broadway, they laughed again in the same places and sometimes in other places, because the truth is that I think that John isn't just an 'Irish writer'. I think there are Irish writers who write in Ireland and there are Irish writers who write and are universal, and I believe John is one of those.

I think Keane follows the tradition of Goldsmith and Boucicault; I think Brian Friel has a few plays that have translated into other countries and a few that simply don't – *Philadelphia, Here I Come*, for instance, works in America and works all over the world; but *Aristocrats* probably doesn't; and *Translations* works, but does it work in America? I don't think so. Authors often hit universal themes but sometimes playwrights come, like Goldsmith and Boucicault and I think like John, who hit a theme and have a particular talent that is so universal it translates everywhere in the world.

I suppose *The Matchmaker* comes down to one of John's main themes, which is about love, and not just love but the interpersonal relationships of people which are bounded by time and space and loneliness and longing, things that are said, and things that aren't said … directly.

In *The Matchmaker*, in our condensed text – the play is maybe sixty per cent of what's in the book – we've distilled for a live audience the salient moments, the important emotional narrative points, without losing the energy and the emphasis. What is interesting I think is that John's work will translate, and is starting to translate worldwide, because he's touching the universal chord that all great plays do: they're about love, they're about contact, they're about loneliness, they're about greed, they're about selfishness; but on a very human level as opposed to being a local level so they're not plays that will date. The reviews for *The Matchmaker* are a case in point. We had thought of *The Matchmaker* as the soufflé as opposed to *Sive*, which is a serious play and will rip the heart of you, or *The Field*. *The Matchmaker* is like a nice cake with nice colours, it's great, it moves you, but it's not a deep play. I'm talking about a man who lived, since 1959, with enormous success and response from audiences in all parts of the country – but his plays, when reviewed in recent years by a number of people who are supposed to be leading theatre critics, have been consistently refused entry to the 'sacred hall of fame' by those very people who would not take cognisance of what John is actually achieving in terms of writing for the theatre in this country.

However, when we took John's work to England and to Scotland we were in an open level playing field, a field (if you'll pardon the pun) where people were saying, 'a writer we don't know'. The leading reviewer in the *London Times* said, 'I'm sorry, I just have to apologise for liking this show: it's simply good old-fashioned theatre. We on the Edinburgh Fringe, we should have people with t-shirts and daggers and cut-throat razors, it should be cutting edge – and the most moving thing I've come across is this production. It's simple, it's moved me – it's old-fashioned theatre and it's amazing.' The review from *The New York Times* said, 'Up the road they've got all these people dressed up as cats and lions in masks and whatever, but down in this tiny theatre off-Broadway magic is happening.'

That magic of John's is about touching humans: John's writing touches you. He touches you in a number of ways and he touches you primarily through his language. If you get the rhythm of the language right, you unveil not just the sentiment of the character but also a whole consciousness of nationhood, a consciousness of what 'Irishness' is, and also of what being 'human' is.

A couple of years ago, I did a translation, with Niall Tobín, of *An Giall /The Hostage* by Brendan Behan, back from the Irish into English and one of the things we were conscious of was that when you write in Irish there's no class: Irish is Irish, there might be a bit of accent but there isn't any class distinction. When we were translating *The Hostage* into English we went back to *An Giall*, the original play and we sought to find a syntax that would be appropriate to who the characters were. For the person who was from Macklesfield, the young hostage, we didn't just translate it literally, we actually went and found how you would speak if you were came from Macklesfield and how the structure of your language would go. Instead of doing a literal translation, we refigured the words so that he had a syntax which was appropriate to how he spoke. John did the same thing, his characters always speak with the right syntax and that is extraordinary: a lot of people write characters but they don't give them a structure within their language that holds up for the whole character; John did that, and was very thorough about it.

It is through his language, in the long run, that he will reach the widest audiences. What we have found is that, taking his work to other countries, we're not afraid of the language anymore. It's a thing to be emphasised: it is poetic language; you are going to find a heightened poetry in the language. Even the prose is structured in a heightened poetic way.

Let me move on to another of John's main themes: 'society'. John wrote *The Field* in 1963–64, with a local murder as its background; but it's bigger play than that. One of the exciting things about *The Field* is that, while the Bull McCabe is a great character in Irish literature and we all know what he does, the other characters who lurk in that play are also very interesting. Maimie in particular is an extraordinary character. Some of John's greatest plays are all about women: there's Moll, there's Big Maggie and there's Maimie in *The Field*. Very few playwrights actually titled plays for women. *Moll* and *Big Maggie* were written for two actresses in particular, but if you look at *The Change in Mame Fadden*, for instance, if you look at *Moll* and *Big Maggie*, he was writing plays about the social order in Ireland when it was not being done.

In *The Field* he's saying that this woman in this play,

Maimie Flanagan, is an abused wife: her husband basically rapes her once a year and they have a child; he doesn't wash ever, he never changes his clothes; he rapes her once a year; she's been down to the priest a couple of times and the priest has effectively told her 'woman go back, and take the beating for the sake of your marriage' – John wrote that in 1964. When the play was produced, many church halls wouldn't have it on because they didn't want the criticism.

At the end of *The Field* Bull tells the priest and the local guard 'it's very simple: there's two of you, lads, and you are the power and we here, we're all the poor small people; if you come here, you don't come down here alone: a guard comes down with the priest or comes down with the doctor, and all of us small people here are mashed in between'. Putting this on the Irish stage in 1965 was extraordinarily courageous. But because this courage is hidden in the idea of a country play and The Abbey would not do it then , he hasn't in fact received the credit for what he achieved socially within Irish drama. He's always tackled difficult subjects. He's hidden them, because he's a clever writer, in what seemed a colloquialism, but in fact he's ruthless about making his point. Look at *The Matchmaker* and you giggle all the way through it but when it comes down to it here's this extraordinary scene where the priest excommunicates the matchmaker, and his wife, in shock, dies. The priest is cold and seemingly ruthless because, as the matchmaker says, 'the only thing you're interested in is the price of the weddings, you're not interested in the people itself.'

John could not stand hypocrisy and he had a number of extraordinary rows with the church and various institutions. It's a central theme of his. One of the things I was doing with *The Field* when we were re-staging it was looking at John's original from Mercier Press. I restored all of the original material, which isn't in the schools' edition, including the conversations with Maimie where she talks about her husband beating her up and abusing her, because I felt this is what John wanted: this wasn't just a play about a man moaning about a field, this is about a society. There's a murder in the background but the man is accidentally murdered so it's not a premeditated murder. The Bull isn't simply a monstrous character, he's man who has a conscience: he finishes the play saying everybody will forget about this – 'except me'. He ends up in grief, in fact in tragedy. He's not terribly far off the Scottish king if he hadn't been chopped up, or Lear. He's a great tragic character because he eventually realises his flaw and this flaw haunts him – forever.

John and I talked about *The Field* for almost eighteen months before I produced and directed it (because the rights weren't available when I wanted to do it and I had to wait a while). We spoke about how he wanted things, what he saw the Bull as, people he'd liked as the Bull, things he didn't like about what had been done.

The Field is a play about social change; it's a play about changing Ireland of the 1960s; about the people coming with the factories, people who had emigrated perhaps in the 1950s to work on the roads, with the bit of money coming back to a changing Ireland. William Dee in *The Field* is about twenty-eight, he went to England when he was about sixteen and he's married now and he runs his own business. He emigrated from Galway in the late 1950s, just after the war, to be a labourer. He was obviously clever enough not just to be a labourer but also to become a foreman, and from becoming the foreman to being able to dress himself in a suit one day, go down to the bank and get the loan to run his own business. He comes back into this rural community of which he isn't a part – he's coming back to his wife's community; his community is Galway – so it's not simply that he's an outsider: he's an Irish person who's an outsider in this community. It's quite intriguing how the Bull addresses him as a 'foreign cock with hair oil' and that's one of the things that really upset him because William Dee says he is an Irish person. None of villagers will take him as an Irish person because he's come back not dressed as they expect an Irish person of his age to be. Irish people of his age, twenty-eight, did not come back to Ireland owning big businesses and want to buy up the land to turn it into a factory.

The Field becomes in fact, not simply a play about a murder, but a play where the Bull sees social change happening, sees the Ireland of the fields and cows turning into an Ireland of the factory and concrete. He is trying to fight to keep the community as he knows it together and he will do anything to do that. He effectively frightens his community through threats, anger, and power and through his personality into keeping quiet so that the community can stay together. But he knows he has stopped the field turning into a concrete thing for the moment, but he hasn't stopped progress.

Throughout the play, the Bull and Maimie are actually the sparring partners. There are two people who stand up to The Bull: one is William Dee and he dies, and eventually the Bull crunches Maimie down saying in effect 'darling it's very simple: you shut your trap and stop opposing me or there's either a bomb at your door or your child … now you take your choice'. Maimie's eldest son Leamy is eventually sent away because he's getting so upset and doesn't want to continue lying. They decide: let's say he had a nervous breakdown and we sent him away. But they're sending the young kid away until the police go away from the town. Maimie has to do that because she realises that the whole society will come crumbling down if they talk. It's fascinating how John has written this accurate portrait of what a small town in the 1960s must have been like – a closed society with the threat of change and how people reacted to that threat of change.

John is also extraordinary in the way he writes about the women in *The Field*. The men discuss the women in the same way they talk about their animals. At one stage, Tadgh's girl-friend is described as 'a fine wedge of a woman, a bit red in the legs', and later on she's described almost as a cow: 'she's a good milker' and all the rest. Maimie stands in the midst of all of this, listening to women being derided publicly by the men and takes them on. She actually stands up to the Bull several times and basically he is saying to her: 'darling, I know enough about you to cause you a great deal of trouble, so shut up or there'll be trouble'. He bullies her, but she takes him on, again and again. Her son Leamy tried to take him on and he's sent away. At the end of the play there's a moment between the Bull and Maimie where what she's really saying is 'I'm keeping my mouth shut here, but it's my choice: you haven't frightened me but I realise that if I have to keep my family together then I need to do this. I'm doing this for my family, I'm not going to be beaten by you'. Maimie is a modern woman.

Then you look at (Big) Maggie, she too runs the business

where her husband *was* the business, and suddenly she becomes the business. She does whatever she does, her way, for the love of the family; and it makes her into a monstrous person. But she realises that she's struggling within the bounds of her society; she's fighting the prejudices in the town where a woman is now running the big business in the town – the travelling salesmen are going to have to come in and see her now, not the husband. It's interesting how John writes about these extraordinarily strong women – how they mature and how they take control of their lives. And John was doing this in the 1960s when nobody else was writing like this. In a sense, John hasn't received a lot of the credit for this because he wasn't presented in the Abbey of the time, or the Gate. In fact, he worked with the people, and his plays have become folkloric plays in that sense because they translated nationwide into people's consciousnesses, because of the manner in which people could relate to the characters, because the situations he picked are universal situations. Would *The Field* have worked in America? I don't see why not because all of America is about land. Would it work in New Guinea? I would think so because the central thing about *The Field* is about land: land in my name is my land; as the Bull says when talking to the priest, 'When you'll be gone Father, to be a Canon somewhere, and the Sergeant gets a wallet of notes and is going to be a Superintendent ... Tadhg's children will be milk-in' cows and keepin' donkeys away from our ditches. That's what we have to think about and if there's no grass then that's the end of me and mine.' That message works in any country in any part of the world at any time. That's the key to what John has caught: he has touched a universal moment in time in all things.

That takes me to my next subject – the lonely heart. The Bull has an extraordinary scene with his son just before they murder William Dee and the big moment is when the son says, 'why don't youself and Ma talk? ... How long has it been?' One of the biggest laughs of the evening is when the Bull says, 'Eighteen years since I slept with her, or spoke to her', and the audience howl with laughter. There's another moment when the policeman interrogates Maimie and the audience are laugh-ing as it goes on: 'didn't he [the Bull] have an argument with the dead man?' and she saying, 'you can't argue with a dead man!' The audience laugh and laugh and right in the middle of all the laughing the priest says, 'you have nothing to tell us?' and Maimie turns and she says, 'what do you think I am? A bloody schoolgirl is it?' The policeman says, 'you were here the night of the murder?' and she replies, 'I'm always here' and she breaks down crying. She actually has a breakdown in front of them all, while the audience are laughing.

John picks these moments which are extraordinarily touching and he makes the audience laugh all round it – and frequently right through somebody having an extraordinarily emotional moment – and you laugh at them, and then as they're actually having the breakdown you realise you're really laughing at human frailty. It touches you in a way that's more interesting than if you had a big tragedy because in fact John doesn't write big tragedies – except perhaps *Sive*, where you come in and there is a dead body at the end – but he doesn't really write the tragedies where the play fades. The Bull ends as a tragedy but the Bull ends as a tragedy in the middle of a room and he goes off and has a pint. The tragedy doesn't stop him living. Whereas in a Shakespearean plays by the time everybody's dead the tragedy's over and the new order takes over, as in *Hamlet*.

One of the trademarks of John as a writer is that he writes very humorously, he invites you into this laughter, he writes great lines which are funny; but he invests those lines with humanity and you are touched by that humanity.

For instance, one of my favourite letters from *The Matchmaker* is from the woman called the 'Murphy girl' who gets enormous laughs. We've worked hard in *The Matchmaker* to keep the characters absolutely human, simple, and true, because I've always felt that if you patronise the people you lose their humanity, and once you unveil their humanity the audience laugh not just because they recognise it but they also become moved by it. The 'Murphy girl' is one of these characters, again like Maimie, who moves you very simply through her absolute innocence and you laugh. Nonetheless, you feel for her because if you give her her own honesty and you don't patronise her, she's extraordinarily sad and lovely, she's very lonely and yet she's found happiness. John also writes about love too: love and happiness. Let me quote a bit from the 'Murphy girl':

The Tailrace,
Feale River Cross.

Dear Mr O'Connor,

I am the Murphy girl from the Tailrace that got married lately to Tom Cuddy of Been Hill. I am enclosing the money that's due to you. All our thanks are due to you too.

We are very happy although 'tis only a month since the knot was tied. Life was so lonely for the two of us especially and we so backward and tuathallach not knowing how to put one word on top of another in the company of strangers. You changed all that and I am sure that there is a happy future before us.

What a shy man and what a grand man and what a loving man is my husband. Politer you wouldn't meet in draper's shop.

The night we got married he was slow about getting down to business, but once he started he gave a good account of himself. He's so mannerly. In the morning he gave me a little tap on the shoulder – 'I beg your pardon, Miss Murphy,' says, he 'but could I trouble you once more.'

Gratefully yours
Catherine Cuddy (Nee Murphy)

Because she's so simple, and so honest she makes you laugh but you're deeply touched by her – that's what John does: he touches you with that loneliness and once he touches the loneliness he makes you laugh and so you laugh, by being opened up. It touches you in a more profound way than just comedy where you just laugh and laugh, as his characters make you laugh because you recognise the ordinariness of them and it's through that ordinariness he becomes a great play-wright as he turns the ordinary into the extraordinary. That's a sign of not just a good play but of an extraordinary play.

Let me quote from *The Year of the Hiker* when the hiker comes back (as you know, the hiker's been off for twenty years, hasn't got on with the sister-in-law or the wife and he comes back):

> *Freda : That'll be a fox.' (and the hiker turns up) …'we had twenty*
> *years of peace – twenty good years move on …'*
> *Hiker: Where's Kate …?*
> *Freda: What's it to you? You're a stranger here.'*
> *Hiker: … Is Kate dead? …*
> *Freda: … I refuse to answer the question … you have no right to ask.*
> *Hiker: Aren't you going to tell me anything about my family?'*
> *Freda: They're not your family anymore. Don't you understand …*
> *you don't belong here.*

(Let us pass now to –)

> *Freda: They're ashamed of you! The very mention of your name*
> *and they start hating you …*

> Hiker: *These twenty years were no fun. I had my pride and there was no coming back for me. Pride is no virtue, but pride can give a man a bit of dignity.*

> Hiker: *... I couldn't make her [Kate] into a woman with you around ... There was no peace and fulfilment in our love-making with you in the house ... Holy people like you should be kept a million miles away from love ...*

> Hiker: *Let me alone! Your God and my God are different people. I came too far to go away again ... Twenty years is enough.*

You can see from this that in his language he's arguing with the 'Holy Marys' – as the hiker echoing Bull McCabe when he says your God and my God aren't the same God. One of the most touching moments in *The Matchmaker* is when the matchmaker's wife dies and he writes about her death: there's bitterness because the priest, effectively, excommunicated him and she dies of shock. You can see in all of the works – you can see it in *The Field* most clearly – that John could not stand hypocrisy and his use of language is extraordinary in dealing with this.

In *The Hiker* you have to take sides – between Freda, the stay-at-home maiden aunt who lives with the sister; Kate, the deserted wife; and the hiker. By making you take sides with the characters, you get angry with them. You observe the continued row with Freda in a focused way:

> Freda: Merciful Mother o' God, can't you leave me alone? ... All
> these years I've hated you ... I was hard and bitter, not like
> other women. I was too wise and sober – not like Kate, she was
> soft and foolish. I couldn't have ogled you even if I'd wanted to
> like other women ... When Kate told me that night that you
> wanted to marry her, it was near being the death of me ...
> Hiker: I never gave you any call to think that I was interested in you,
> beyond you were Kate's sister.
> Freda: ... You did, you did. You used to rip the strings of my apron
> for devilment and you kissed me, you kissed me ... you often
> kissed me.
> Hiker: That was before I proposed to Kate and I teased you and I
> kissed you because you were Kate's sister and Kate was the girl
> I loved ...

You're propelled into this row between this threesome: the
two sisters, the one who was chosen and the other who wasn't
and how one turned against the other, and you wonder, 'is it
just about a row?' But no, this is a play about the fact that
twenty, thirty, forty years beforehand the land laws changed
all of these people were left at home. The idle person, or the
person who wasn't married: what did this person do? And so
you find that *The Year of the Hiker* isn't simply a play about a
man wandering the road but in fact it becomes a social play:
John is writing about the fact that Ireland changed, changed
from being a rural society into being a modern society; about
the nuclear family. It's a bit like Mena in *Sive*: she wants her
family, her husband and herself without the granny in the
way. In the same way here: can Freda be married and not married to the Hiker, can there be this threesome of some kind?

She's a bit like the cuckoo in the nest. John was writing about how society has changed: these are the left over moments that we know. We all know of some situation where the maiden aunt or the uncle, or the brother is left in the house with the married couple and there's always the tension that is about the married couple wanting to be alone and have a life. My mother had a sister who lived with them and she was, not unlike Freda, the extra person in the marriage; and only when she died, about five years ago, did my parents actually get to know each other again and a new intimacy grew back between them.

John, writing that in the 1960s, was ahead of his time. One of the reviews of Edinburgh from one of the leading newspapers in England said, 'where has this playwright been: he's one of these undiscovered people, he's a playwright we don't know, his works are missing in English literature.' I hope we'll be able to change this over the coming years: that we can bring his works alive not simply in this country but give him the credit as a writer that he's due.

Let me quote a couple more pieces from *The Matchmaker*. Fionnuala Crust is the opposite of the 'Murphy girl': she's extremely difficult. She's about sixty and alone, and she's not afraid to admit she's alone. She's written to the Matchmaker and he writes back saying he has somebody. She replies:

Dear Dicky,

The sooner the better.

After the non-starter you fobbed over on me the last time, I would be well entitled to the best you have.

O'Connor's snug in Killarney would suit me fine. There's buses back and forth the whole time between Coomasahara and Killarney.

Some of them bus drivers are fine able men, well fleshed and solid. 'Tis my guess that they'd be lively at night over they being sitting down all day.

This Carrolane you have for me sounds like a likely mark. I would be most anxious to leave no grass grow so fix the meeting for soon.

I have only one life and the Catechism don't say nothing about courting or coupling in the hereafter.

I don't want to die without the imprint of a man.

Make the meeting for Sunday week or for the Sunday after at the latest.

Fionnuala Crust (Miss)

The centre of that letter is about loneliness and she's not afraid to admit it. One of the great things is that you laugh through all of that, but the after-taste lingers. It isn't just funny: it's funny because you recognise it, you recognise the longing. It's so compact as a piece of writing.

The same craftsman wrote this (after his wife has died, the matchmaker writes):

Dear Jack,

The black times are back again. I was never so low in myself in all my days. She was the light of my life and the pulse of my heart. My heart breaks for her ... You have no way, Jack, of knowing the

> meaning of grief until it lifts the latch on your own door. I remember
> Kate and me was coming home one summer's evening from the
> meadow when the sky was blackened and the rain came down. We
> took shade in under an old sycamore tree in the corner of the haggard
> … Soon the sun came out …. and the birds started singing …
>
> Kate took my hand and this is what she said.
>
> 'Isn't it grand for you and me Dicky,' says she. 'Isn't it surely
> grand for me and you.'
>
> … She'll never call me again for my supper nor bring the tay to
> the meadows in the summer. I had great times entirely with her.
>
> God knows the value of her. 'Twas he took her.

Here John is also writing about the relationship he had with Mary, his wife, because without Mary he wouldn't have been able to do what he did. You find John writing about his relationship with his children, with his town, his life. In his writings, it's submerged and hidden. What Dicky is saying about his wife, is what John is saying about his own life, which is something you all recognise from somewhere in your own past. It's the simple things that move you, it's the tiny ones and that's characteristic of John's writing. In those small moments, he catches you unawares. And again John B., ahead of his time, tackled themes about abused wives, about the widow left alone, the change of life, etc., and here he has a Claude Glynn-Hunter in *The Matchmaker* writing:

Hunter Hall,
Ballyninty,
Co. Limerick.

Sir,

Many thanks for your letter. I note what you say about the difficulty of procuring young wives these days. Perhaps I was a bit too choosy … you may now widen the net in the hope of attracting marriageable dames from the age of thirty-five downwards. This should not be too difficult … meanwhile would you know of any nice boy who would like a good home. The work would be light and I promise to be very fond of him. Any sweet boy under forty would suit nicely.

I will be spending Christmas with my married sister in England but will be back for the New Year when I hope no doubt you will have some cheering news for me.

Yours cordially,
Claude Glynn-Hunter

In a sense, you find John touching something which other writers did not do until the late 1980s when people started writing about the need in people to have alternative relationships. He writes very movingly about a character called Cornelius J. McCarthy. I want to quote a contrast to it from *Sharon's Grave*. Both of these are about social comments, both of these about language, both are about the lonely heart: all three are interlinked. The first is Dinzie, who is the cripple in *Sharon's Grave* (they want him to go out of the house and he says):

I won't go out of here! I won't go out of here, I've no legs to be travelling the country with. I must have my own place. I do be crying

and cursing myself at night in bed because no woman will talk to me.
I puts my nails to my flesh because no girl will ever look at me on
account of my dead legs … And this impostor here … this hound of
the devil, this curse o' God on my back …

That's John writing about a cripple. I think Dinzie talks later
about always dreaming of women and being lonely but he's a
violent, nasty man; he's hurt, he's very wounded and he's very
aggressive in his wounds. Whereas Cornelius says:

> *Menafreghane*
> *Tullylore*
> *Co. Cork*

Dear Mr O'Connor,

*I am what people call a cripple. All that's wrong with me is that I
have a wasted leg and a bit of a permanent stoop. I swear to you I
haven't spoken to ten women in my lifetime. I am no good to con-
verse with them, and I am not a success at dances as you can well
imagine on account of my disabilities … I need a wife and have almost despaired of ever getting one …*

*I am aged forty-one, and you are the last straw as far as I am
concerned. I have a nice little farm, a good house but very little
money … I like books and magazines and I have a keen interest in
gardening.*

In God's name Mr O'Connor can you do anything for me?

*All I want is a decent woman around my own age or a little bit
older. I am not worried whether she has money or not. I am not
worried about looks …*

*Please show this letter to no one, and I beg of you to do what
you can for me.*

Yours in hope,
Cornelius J. McCarthy

He moves you beautifully there. It's a wonderful portrait of loneliness and hope and loss. What is extraordinary about his letters is that each of them is like a complete essay, it's a portrait of a character, and it's a play in its own right. Cornelius writes only two letters and he finishes by saying:

> Menafreghane
> Tullylore
> Co. Cork
>
> Dear Mr O'Connor,
>
> *I suppose you could find nobody for me. Remember me? I'm the man with the wasted leg and the stoop. I knew it wouldn't be easy on account of my disability ... For God's sake, do what you can for me as I can find no words to tell you about the loneliness. Hoping to hear from you at your nearest convenience.*
>
> *Yours in hope,*
> *Cornelius J. McCarthy.*

These people all talk about loneliness and they're so honest. From this portrait of Cornelius, you know him: you've seen somebody like him or you know somebody in a house down the road who lives alone and fits the same bill. John caught these people but he was passionate and caring in his portraits. That isn't just about a man who's lonely: he talks about the way the world treats him and how cripples are dealt with.

One of the things I'm interested in doing is opening up into the twentieth-first century a digital repertoire, we're going to bring out an audiotape of John reading his own Christmas stories. We're also bringing out a videotape to go with *The Field*, like *Cole's Notes* used to be. When you want to do schools' notes on *The Field*, you'll get the CD-ROM or the video, you'll pop it in and get the interviews with the actors, you'll find people talking about the central things in the play, how the play works. If over the next few years we can start to treat John as a very serious playwright, as a playwright who deserves our attention, just like Boucicault and Goldsmith, we will be doing not just a service to John but to Irish literature.

When you look back at the structures of John's plays, they follow frequently many of the structures of the Boucicault melodramas. People often think of melodrama as an old thing but in fact no, melodrama is a liberating structure to work in. It defines the rules, so once you know you're at a melodrama you know this is how this fits; so you give up the struggle. *Sive* is a melodrama: there's that wonderful moment when the letter is put on the mantelpiece and you're going, 'don't leave the letter there, she's going to burn it!' It's actually like a moment from a thriller: the tension is extraordinary. The melodrama is set up: you actually believe these people because John's portraits of the people have been so vivid that you recognise them and that involves you in the melodrama in a way that going to see *What Lies Beneath* does not. You're never going to become deeply involved with the people in something like that: you might recognise them but you don't become intimately involved. John wrote these characters whom we recognise as a culture, but what I'm finding is that other cultures recognise them too, because he's touched that central universal chord.

There're only two people in *The Matchmaker* and they have different accents and it's all about the tone, where those people come from. John has this wicked sense of humour: he writes these addresses and various things in his novellas so that you get the sense of devilment that the man had. I remember one of the great days we were in the pub and he was looking at the pictures on the walls and he said, 'you know, these pictures are a testament to my growing baldness. My whole life is there, summed up: going bald.' It's extraordinary how that remark summed up for him, in a wry way, his life. It wasn't a waste; he just had an odd way of looking at it.

Let me finish with a piece from Tull Macadoo, who is the successful TD. This brings in language and social comment but not, perhaps, the lonely heart. It's Tull Macadoo, writing to his son:

Dear Mick,

There's no doubt but the world is full of gangsters and crooks, as soon you'll all find out. Their numbers grow and grow and it isn't easy to make an honest shilling ...

The trouble with Flannery is that he doesn't understand poli-

tics. I'll have to retire sometime, I suppose – but not yet, by God, not yet – and when that day comes, mark my words, whoever takes over from me will be as true to the party line as I am. There's a word for it ... ethos, that's it ... the party Ethos. It comes down from the top. Where was I? Oh yeah – there are eight hundred and fifty-seven votes in Kilnavarna and if the work on the new road starts on time – and I'll make sure it does – I can safely say I'll get five hundred of them in the October election. That's politics around these parts. I never did well in Kilnavara as you know ...

There you go: I think that's John at his funniest.

USING JOHN B. KEANE IN THE PRIMARY SCHOOL

Gabriel Fitzmaurice

Using John B. Keane in the primary school: we as teachers immediately think of the value of such an enterprise to our pupils. This, I feel, is a mistake – we are thinking about our pupils only; we don't think of ourselves enough. We should think of enriching ourselves too (heaven knows we need a bit of enrichment and nourishment in our lives; otherwise we become frustrated, disillusioned, burnt out).

John B. Keane can be a source of such enrichment, such nourishment for both teacher and pupil. He has proved through the years that literature can reach everyone from the groves of academe to the parish pump. He has packed city theatres and village halls the length and breadth of Ireland and beyond. In doing so, he has proved the value of the local, the indispensability of the local. He has shown us how the local is universal. He has done so using a local dialect – the rich language of his beloved North Kerry, the love child, as he was wont to contend, of Elizabethan English and our native Gaelic.

I want to look at John B. Keane from the perspective of

a primary teacher in the classroom faced with ordinary Irish children of the present generation who, it is commonly held, are more interested in PlayStations and DVDs than they are in books.

For a while, I thought books were losing out; I thought that the computer would replace the book – but then along came Harry Potter striking a mighty blow for the solitary reader. I shouldn't have been despondent however. In 1998 on the day that Bryan MacMahon died, I read my class his 'Jacko-moora and the King of Ireland's Son', a local folk tale retold from the Gaelic by the Master himself. The children were spellbound. At the end of the story there was an audible sigh of pure pleasure from the children who admitted to me that they enjoyed the story better than anything they had seen on television. That is the power of story. That is why the book will never die. (Indeed, might I add in passing, that the motto of the Listowel Drama Group which introduced John B. Keane when they premiered his *Sive* in 1959, and which also produced many of Bryan MacMahon's plays, is 'The Stage Shall Never Die'. Such is the optimism of North Kerry when it comes to literary matters, surely one of the reasons it has produced, and continues to produce, writers of substance and standing).

The 1971 curriculum for national schools enshrined the

concept of cross-curricular integration. The 1999 curriculum likewise places a huge emphasis on integration. I want to look at John B. Keane in this context. You will find that his work lends itself to such an approach. Integration, I find, is an ideal way for the teacher to find expression in the classroom. Integration is personal and allows the individual teacher to choose among subjects and themes thereby putting a personal stamp on the curriculum. Teachers should claim ownership of what they teach. One of the central tenets of the 1999 curriculum (and I was part of the team that drew up the English component of that curriculum) is that the teacher should be enabled, not enslaved, by the curriculum. The teacher should be enabled to explore the excitement, the beauty, the challenge of educating children (and, *ipso facto*, themselves), beginning with the local and proceeding to the universal. *Ní lia daoine ná tuairimí* as the *seanfhocal* goes – no two people think exactly alike. So different teachers will approach integration differently.

What follows is my personal 'take' on a few aspects of John B. Keane's work which, I submit, would be suitable for the national school. I want to look at John B. Keane under the following headings: travellers, place, emigration, fathers and sons.

Travellers come into the curriculum under a variety of

headings: we meet them in the religion programme, we meet them in history, in geography, in social and environmental studies, in English and Gaeilge. At a time when racism is a live issue in this country, it is well to consider our own native racist issue. Our attitude to travellers needs examining. They are blamed for crime in this country no matter that most crimes emanate from the settled community; they are blamed for drunkenness and brawling – look at the streets of our cities and towns at weekends: it isn't travellers who are drunk and disorderly there but the sons and daughters of the settled community. A writer's duty is to go beyond the common perception of things. This may make the writer unpopular, but that is what a writer has to do. John B. Keane and many other writers, his fellow townsman Bryan MacMahon included, have gone beyond the prejudice, the hostility of the settled community towards the traveller. John B. served travellers in his pub. He did so not only out of a sense of justice and fair play, but because he could tap into their culture, their lore, the otherness of their way of life. Indeed this is what he used to do with the settled community too. As one astute observed remarked to John B. early in his writing career, 'You takes down what we says and you charges us to read it!' In giving the tinkers (I use the term without prejudice) Pats Bocock and his poet-son Carthalawn a central role in *Sive*, he not only allows them to comment on the action, he gives us an other view, a tinker's (for which read outsider's) view, a poet's view of society. The tinker and the poet are one in the character of Carthalawn. Indeed, Seán Dota, speaking for the settled community, says of poets: 'I have nothing against the poets, mind you, but they are filled with roguery and they have the bad tongue on top of it, the thieves'. Like poet, like tinker to the settled folk.

By way of illustration (and this would ideally suit the classroom) I want to look at Carthalawn's cursing verses from *Sive*. Note the power, the eloquence, and the just-so-right quality of the invective that hits the target spot-on:

> *May the snails devour his corpse*
> *And the rain do harm worse*
> *May the devil sweep the hairy creature soon;*
> *He's as greedy as a sow,*
> *As the crow behind the plough*
> *The black man from the mountain, Seánín Rua.*
>
> *May he screech with awful thirst*
> *May his brains and eyeballs burst*
> *That melted amadán, that big bostoon,*
> *May the fleas consume his bed*
> *And the mange eat up his head,*
> *The black man from the mountain, Seánín Rua.*

In passing might I add that cursing has been the prerogative of poets from ancient times. In our own time, local poets have cursed memorably too. One thinks of Paddy Drury's (though some dispute that it was his):

Knockanure both mane and poor
Has a church without a steeple
And bitches and hoors looking out half-doors
Criticising dacent people.

Or Michael Hartnett's

Abbeyfeale is a fair old place,
Kilmorna wouldn't grow a haw;
Lyreacrompane is the worst place of all —
but f*** me, Duagh!

Now listen to two travellers telling their tale. Nan Joyce in her poem 'The Wild Trabler' (i.e., 'The Wild Traveller' rendered here into standard English by Leland Bardwell) paints a bleak picture far removed from the 'Níl fear in Éirinn chomh meidhreach, aerach/ Leis an tincéir Sás Ó Néill' nonsense we were once upon a time force-fed in our schooldays:

THE WILD TRAVELLER

The Wild Traveller. The wild traveller
Is a man that fights when he is drunk
And always shouting, that people think
He is full of hate. But no,
Just a man that life left behind
A man who never had a chance in life
Since he was born. Unwanted, outcast
In his own country since he was a child
He was rejected, living wild like the birds
Being hunted like a wild animal.
People snarl at him and are afraid of him.
Life never brought him any happiness.
He curses the day he was born.

He sometimes asks God why he was put on earth.
He is an unhappy man who never had a true friend
Then he turns to the only friend he has. The friend
That makes him laugh and cry and happy for a while
A friend that will bring him closer to death.
This is a wild man.

Pecker Dunne's song 'Wexford' is at once a hymn to and a criticism of his native place as all the best such balladry should be:

My family lived in Wexford town,
Stopped travelling and settled down;
Though my father kept a horse and car(t),
We lived within the town;
The people there misunderstood,
They did not know our ways,
So with horse and car(t) back on the road
I began my travelling days.

My father was called The Fiddler Dunne
And I'm a fiddler too;
Although I often felt his fist,
He taught me all he knew;
I know I'll never be as good
And yet I feel no shame,
For the other things my father taught,
I am proud to bear his name.

He taught me pride and how to live
Though the road is hard and long,
And how a man will never starve
With a banjo, fiddle or a song,
And how to fight for what I own
And what I feel is right,
And how to camp beside a ditch
On a stormy winter's night.

Oh! times were good and times were bad
And people cruel and kind;
But what I learned of people then
Has stayed within my mind;
I'll honour friends with all my heart,
Do for them all I can,
But I've learned to go the road again
Where they spurn a tinker man.

Oh! Wexford is a town I like
But the travelling man they scorn
And a man must feel affection
For the town where he was born;
I know one day that I'll go back
When my travelling days are done
And people will begin to wonder
What has happened to the Pecker Dunne?

Under the heading of travellers one might also investigate works like Bryan MacMahon's 'The Honey Spike', 'A Woman's Hair' or 'What the Tinker Woman Said to Me'; Sigerson Clifford's 'The Ballad of the Tinker's Son' or 'The Ballad of the Tinker's Wife'; Ewan MacColl's 'Travelling People' or his 'Moving-on Song' to mention but a few.

John B. Keane loved his native place, Listowel. He wrote about its people, their fables and their foibles, their greatness and their pettiness, their culture and their character. In his poem 'The Street' (see p. 79), he paints a loving picture of his native Church Street. His great friend, the poet Michael Hartnett, has painted a rather different picture of his native street, Maiden Street in Newcastle West, Co. Limerick. He clearly loves his native place. In his poem 'Maiden Street Ballad' he writes:

> But what can I say of a small country town
> that is not like Killarney, known all the world round?
> that has not for beauty won fame or renown
> but still all the same is quite charming?
> I have seen some fine cities in my traveller's quest,
> put Boston and London and Rome to the test
> but I wouldn't give one foot of Newcastle West
> for all of their beauty and glamour

But he cannot ignore the money-grabbing gombeenism of certain traders in the town who preyed on the poverty the community experienced in Maiden Street:

> Now before you get settled, take a warning from me
> for I'll tell you some things that you won't like to hear –
> we were hungry and poor down in Lower Maiden Street,
> a fact I will swear on the Bible.
> There were shopkeepers then, quite safe and secure –
> seven masses a week and then shit on the poor:
> ye know who I mean, of that I am sure,
> and if they like, they can sue me for libel.
>
> They say you should never speak ill of the dead,
> but a poet must say what is inside his head –
> let drapers and bottlers now tremble in dread:
> they no longer can pay men slave wages.
> Let hucksters and grocers and traders join in
> for they all bear the guilt of a terrible sin:
> they thought themselves better than their fellow-men –
> now the nettles grow thick on their gravestones.

But there are moments of great beauty too:

Go out some fine evening, walk up to the Park
when the sun shines on Rooska and the Galtees are dark
and all the nice gardens are tidy and smart
and the dogs lie asleep in the roadway:
and the blue of the hills with their plumes of white smoke
in a hazy half-circle do shelter our homes
and the crows to the treetops fly home in black rows
and the women wheel out their new go-cars.

When the children in dozens are playing at ball
and Dick Fitz and Mike Harte stand and chat by the wall
and a hundred black mongrels do bark and do brawl
and scratch their backsides in the street there:
when the smell of black pudding it sweetens the air
and the scent of back rashers it spreads everywhere
and the smoke from the chimneys goes fragrant and straight
to the sky in the Park in the evening.

In his preface to 'Maiden Street Ballad', he alludes to John Steinbeck's 'Cannery Row': 'For a good many years people have asked me to write about Maiden Street, to produce a kind of "Cannery Row": this is the closest I could get to it. I used the metre of "The Limerick Rake", the best Hiberno-English ballad ever written in this county. I have not hesitated to use all the conventions of such a song'. Incidentally, when Tom Steinbeck, John Steinbeck's son, lectured at Writers' Week in Listowel shortly after John B. Keane's death, he informed the gathering that John Steinbeck not only knew John B. Keane's plays, but that he was a big fan of Keane's.

Emigration is another theme of John B.'s. In plays like *Many Young Men of Twenty* he examines emigration, its causes and effects. A sometime emigrant himself, he knows, understands and sympathises with the emigrant Irish, particularly in England where he spent some time himself. Here is his ballad 'Many Young Men of Twenty' from the play:

Many young men of twenty said goodbye
All that long day,
From break of dawn till the sun was high
Many young men of twenty said goodbye.

My boy, Jimmy, went that day
On the big ship sailed away
Sailed away and left me here to die
Many young men of twenty said goodbye.

My Jimmy said he'd sail across the sea
He swore his oath,
He'd sail again, back home to marry me
My Jimmy said he'd sail across the sea
But my Jimmy left me down
O, my Jimmy, please come back to me!
O, my Jimmy, please come back to me!

Many young men of twenty said goodbye
It breaks my heart, to see the face of girl and boy
It breaks my heart and now I'm fit to die

My boy Jimmy's gone from me
Sailed away across the sea
Jimmy's gone and here alone am I
Many young men of twenty said goodbye

Many young men of twenty said goodbye
All that long day,
From break of dawn till the sun was high
Many young men of twenty said goodbye

They left the mountain and the glen
The lassies and the fine young men
I saw the tears of every girl and boy

Many young men of twenty said goodbye
Many young men of twenty said goodbye.

Áine Ní Ghlinn, writing in Irish, has a similar feel for the Irish emigrant in England. Here are a few extracts from her 'Páidín' sequence which I translated into English:

PÁIDÍN

It isn't Páidín or Pat
or even Paddy
he calls himself
now
that he's in London
but Patrick
Patrick Conneely
and he didn't even look
over his shoulder
the time
he heard
the woman shouting
'Páidín'
that morning
he was standing
backside to the wind
at the hiring fair
in Cricklewood
'I'm not Páidín'
he insisted to himself
'but Patrick
Patrick Conneely'
His neck scragged
to loosen

a non-existent tie
Him like an old cow
chewing the cud
trying to get his tongue around
'Patrick
Patrick Conneely'

CRICKLEWOOD 6.00 A.M.

Everyone has their own version of things
And it's the same with Páidín Ó Conaola
Or – excuse me – Patrick Conneely
'Between jobs I am' he says
'You know yourself and I thought that since
I'd nothing else to do
I might as well come down here
in hopes that I'd meet someone –
someone from home – you know yourself
No No – It's not shortage of work or money
Just – Well, you know yourself'

ANOTHER DAY DOWN

Páidín stands at the counter
laughs at the smutty story
he tells himself
In a soft voice he talks dirty
to a woman who walks away

He makes a fist of his right hand
punches the air
getting the better
of that big bastard of an Englishman
who called him a Paddy this morning

His left hand pumps in the beer
This stuff isn't as good

as the beer in Ireland
but anyway it's
'Another pint, my good man'

At closing time
Páidín bids goodbye
to the barman
to the strangers
to his imagined friends

He walks around the corner
Pisses
against the wall
pukes the night's beer

Then, singing Amhrán na bhFiann,
he walks back to his poky room
kisses the photo of his mother
takes off his boots
and sleeps

A VISIT HOME

Páidín drove home for Christmas
in a car whose front bumper would be
at the church door
while the back wheels
were still coming in the gate
He kept the documents
from the car rental company
hidden deep down
in the inside pocket
of his Sunday jacket

Dominic Behan has written many fine emigration ballads as have Seán McCarthy and a host of other ballad singers. These, and other, ballads and poems bound the Irish community together both at home and abroad much as singing and playing the blues helped the black people of America to articulate and overcome their troubles in life.

John B. Keane loved his parents, in particular his father, a national teacher with a love of books and alcohol. He writes about his father thus:

When he spoke gustily and sincerely
Spittle fastened
Not merely upon close lapel
But nearly blinded
Those who had not hastened
To remove pell-mell.
He was inviolate.
Clung to old stoic principle,
And he
Dismissed his weaknesses
As folly.
His sinning was inchoate;
Drank ill-advisedly.
His waistcoat I remember –
Tobacco-perfumed parallelogram
Of pennied pockets.
Once when unexpected telegram
Advised immediate payment
Eyes rocketed in sockets
At demand of claimant.
He wired this cant:
'Coffers rent apart.
An intimate friend
Of Weller, Tony.
Have ripped beadles apart.
Am, sir, compelled to dial
The number of your heart.'
I am terribly proud of my father,
Bitterly, faithfully proud.

Let none say a word to my father
Or mention his name out loud.
I adored his munificent blather
Since I was his catch-as-catch-can.
I am terribly proud of my father
For he was a loveable man.

I, too, have tried to write about my father, a small farmer's son who ran a grocery shop in the village of Moyvane all the while caring for his invalid wife, my mother, until her death in 1974. Here is my poem:

DAD

A man before his time, he cooked and sewed,
Took care of me – and Mammy in her bed,
Stayed in by night and never hit the road.
I remember well the morning she was dead
(I'd been living up in Arklow – my first job,
I hit the road in patches coming home),
He came down from her room, began to sob
'Oh Gabriel, Gabriel, Gabriel, Mam is gone'.
He held me and I told him not to cry
(I loved her too, but thought this not the place –
I went up to her room, cried softly 'Why?'
Then touched her head quite stiffly, no embrace).
Now when the New Man poses with his kid,
I think of all the things my father did.

The Listowel area has produced writers, many of them writers of substance and standing, for a long time now. John B. Keane continued the play-writing tradition of George Fitzmaurice in terms of both theme and language. He adapted the melodrama and the folk play to the modern stage using the rich dialect of North Kerry. He brought his place and its people to national, even international, attention. He lit the way for a new generation of North Kerry writers, myself included. Because he presented often complex issues in the simplest terms, he has proved that accessibility (despite some critics who hold a contrary view) is a strength and not a weakness. Because of this accessibility, he is an ideal author to be shared between teacher and pupil to the benefit of all.

THE CONTRIBUTORS

Danny Hannon is a native of Listowel and a life-long friend of the
Keane family, he has shared in many of the highlights of John
B.'s career and was usually the chauffeur on the opening nights
of the plays; has also produced several of the plays for the
Lartigue Theatre and adapted other works for Pub Theatre,
performed in John B.'s pub during the summer months.

Fintan O'Toole is a columnist with *The Irish Times*. His books include *The Irish Times Book of the Century, Shakespeare is Hard
but so is Life, A Traitor's Kiss: The Life of Richard Brinsley Sheri-
dan* and *The Lie of the Land*.

Nóra Relihan was a founder of Writers' Week in Listowel and is
founder/chairperson of St John's Theatre and Arts Centre in
Listowel. She served on The Arts Council from 1979 to 1983.
She has acted in many plays and has scripted and performed
her own shows.

Michael Scott is an independent theatre producer and director. He
has been Theatre Director of the Projects Arts Centre, Programme Director of the Dublin Theatre Festival, Director of
the Tivoli Theatre, Dublin and RHA Downstairs. He is cur-
rently Artistic Director of SFX City Theatre.

Pat Moore and *Paddy McElligott* were both born on small farms in Asdee, north Kerry. One has two children and the other has none. Both love living in north Kerry and are interested in people and drama.

Gabriel Fitzmaurice has been teaching in Moyvane National School since 1975 and he is now the principal. He is the author of more than 30 books, including collections of poetry in English and Irish and for children. He frequently broadcasts on radio and television on education and the arts.

DURANGO

JOHN B. KEANE

Danny Binge peered into the distance and slowly spelled out the letters inscribed on the great sign in glaring red capitals:

'DURANGO,' he read.

'That is our destination,' the Rector informed his friend. 'I'm well known here. These people are my friends and before the night is over they shall be your friends too.'

The friends in question are the Carabim girls: Dell, aged seventy-one and her younger sister, seventy-year-old Lily. Generous, impulsive and warm-hearted, they wine, dine and entertain able-bodied country boys free of charge – they will have nothing to do with the young men of the town or indeed any town ...

Durango is an adventure story about life in rural Ireland during the Second World War. It is a story set in an Ireland that is fast dying but John B. Keane, with his wonderful skill and humour, brings it to life, rekindling in the reader memories of a time never to be quite forgotten ...

THE CELEBRATED LETTERS
OF
JOHN B. KEANE

I grew up in a time when there was no alternative to the letter as a means of communication except, of course, in the case of emergency when the phone in the local barracks of the Civic Guards became the extreme resort …

In this collection of some of his finest letters, John B. Keane turns the letter as a means of communication into a comic, sometimes surreal, artform.

Includes *Letters of a Successful TD, Letters of an Irish Parish Priest, Letters of a Love-Hungry Farmer, Letters of a Matchmaker* and *Letters of an Irish Minister of State.*

'Hilariously Irish, shrewdly accurate and richly creative.'

Irish Times

'There are more shades to his humour than there are colours in the rainbow.'

The Examiner

CELEBRATED LETTERS VOL II
OF
JOHN B. KEANE

Includes *Letters of a Civic Guard, Letters of an Irish Publican, Letters of a Country Postman* and *Letters to the Brain.*

The Best

of

John B. Keane
Collected Humorous Writings

John B. Keane is known nationally and internationally as a successful playwright, handling tragedy and comedy with equal art, and as a prose fiction writer of great invention and skill. Yet an equal claim to fame is made by the hundreds of short pieces which have been published in more than dozen highly popular collections, their titles ranging from polemical to surreal, from *Inlaws and Outlaws* to *Is the Holy Ghost Really a Kerryman?* Now harvested into a single volume, they represent the distillation of the experience of a funny, witty, wise and passionate observer of the bright tapestry of Irish life.

All human life is there, and he tells its story in a remarkable procession of remarkable characters. There are mouth-watering disquisitions on food and paeans to drink, and since Kerry people do not live by bread alone, there is much about their two other preoccupations – love and words. *The Best of John B. Keane* is a collection to prize and an ideal bedside book or travelling companion.

MANY YOUNG MEN OF TWENTY
MOLL & THE CHASTITUTE

JOHN B. KEANE

Many Young Men of Twenty, a musical play, deals with emigration and the lack of jobs at home that forced people to leave their native land for England. It describes the emigrants' longing for home, their annual homecomings and their return to jobs and places they dislike.

Moll is a hilarious and highly successful comedy about life in an Irish country presbytery. 'When a presbytery gets a new housekeeper it becomes like a country that gets a change of government, or like a family that gets a new stepmother'. Moll Kettle would work for no less than a canon for, in her own words, ''tis hard to come back to the plain black and white when one is used to the purple'.

In *The Chastitute* John B. Keane holds some 'sacred cows' up to ridicule. 'A chastitute is a person without holy orders who has never lain down with a woman, a rustic celibate by force of circumstance peculiar to countrysides where the Catholic tradition of long-life sexual abstemiousness is encouraged ... free-range sex is absolutely taboo ...'

THE STREET
Poems and Ballads

JOHN B. KEANE

This expanded version of *The Street* also includes songs and ballads such as 'Many Young Men of Twenty' and 'Kitty Curley'.

John B. Keane wrote poems at different times in his life. As a young man, he wrote quite a lot, but as he turned his attention more and more to plays, his poetic output understandably diminished. Yet he always kept in touch.

This new collection has all the imaginative vitality and variety, the linguistic energy, the blend of humour and compassion, the sharp powers of observation, the love of nature, the understanding of people, the love of music, the lifelong appreciation of drink and drinking companions, and that tolerant open-mindedness towards different kinds of experience that characterises all his work. Readers of this book, these poems, ballads and songs, will be struck, once again, by the warm humanity of the man who wrote them, and by the scrupulous, traditional skills with which he expressed that humanity.

From the introduction by Brendan Kennelly

Dan Paddy Andy
The Matchmaker

John B. Keane

At a time when priests patrolled the narrow country lanes at night searching with sticks, and even with dogs, for courting couples, Dan Paddy Andy, the matchmaker, came in for ringing denunciations from the Church. Archdeacon Browne intoned from the pulpit: 'There is a wild man after descending from the mountains and it is the man of the triple name: Dan Paddy Andy.'

John B. Keane, master storyteller, paints a colourful and humorous portrait of Dan Paddy Andy, the last of the great Irish matchmakers, who claimed responsibility for over 400 marriages. His wit and escapades are magnificently described by a writer with the accomplished playwright's ear for the subtle tones and vivacity of dialogue.